TV, SCIENCE, and KIDS

TEACHING OUR CHILDREN TO QUESTION

Editorial Advisory Board

ACTION FOR CHILDREN'S TELEVISION (ACT) is a national, nonprofit child advocacy group that works to encourage diversity in children's television and eliminate commercial abuses targeted to children. Founded in 1968, ACT has more than 20,000 national members and the support of major organizations concerned with children.

Action for Children's Television wishes to thank the following corporations and corporate foundations, without whose generous support this book would not have been possible.

> Cabot Corporation Foundation, Inc.
> Cummins Engine Foundation
> Digital Equipment Corporation
> The Pfizer Foundation
> Polaroid Foundation, Inc.
> TRW Foundation
> United Technologies Corporation
> Xerox Corporation

TV, SCIENCE, and KIDS

TEACHING OUR CHILDREN TO QUESTION

Action for Children's Television
Edited by Kim Hays

Foreword by Lewis Thomas, M.D.

ADDISON-WESLEY PUBLISHING COMPANY
READING, MASSACHUSETTS • MENLO PARK, CALIFORNIA
WOKINGHAM, BERKSHIRE • AMSTERDAM • SYDNEY
DON MILLS, ONTARIO

Library of Congress Cataloging in Publication Data
Main entry under title:

TV, science, and kids.

Bibliography: p.
Includes index.
1. Science—Study and teaching (Elementary)—Audiovisual aids—Addresses, essays, lectures. 2. Television
in education—Addresses, essays, lectures.   I. Hays, Kim.
II. Action for Children's Television.   II. Title: T.V.,
science, and kids.
LB1585.T8   1984   372.3'5044   84-12424
ISBN 0-201-06420-0

Copyright © 1984 by Action for Children's Television

Cover design by Marshall Henrichs
Text design by Kenneth Wilson
Set in 10 point Raleigh by P&M Typesetting, Inc., Waterbury, CT.

ISBN 0-201-06420-0

ABCDEFGHIJ-DO-8654

ACKNOWLEDGMENTS

My warmest thanks for their time and thoughtfulness are divided between my colleagues at Action for Children's Television and the authors of these essays. To ACT president Peggy Charren, I offer deeply felt thanks not only for her advice on this book but also for her confidence in me during my years at ACT. I particularly want to recognize the contributions of several ACT staff members: Cynthia Alperowicz, who recommended many excellent changes in the manuscript and then worked to turn it into an attractive book; Susan Siefer, who typed all the related correspondence and many of the essays; and Paula Rohrlick, who prepared the appendixes. In addition, Paula stayed abreast of current science-related newspaper and magazine articles, pursued photographs and their elusive credit lines, and researched the answers to innumerable questions. I have appreciated her help every step of the way.

Among the contributors to the book are several people to whom I am especially grateful for their advice: Fred Jerome, Phil and Phylis Morrison, and George Tressel. Thanks also to Robin McElheny for her thoughtful suggestions.

While working on this book I thought back many times to the people who helped me grow up comfortable with science, and so I think it is only fitting that I acknowledge, with much affection, my chemistry, physics, biology, and general science teachers in grades seven through twelve: Guillermo Castro, Ron McQueen, David Urquhart, and in particular Asunción Rivera de Armstrong.

Finally, my love and thanks to my uncle, Kimball Kramer, a physicist whose many skills and interests prove that C. P. Snow's two cultures need not be at loggerheads.

CONTENTS

FOREWORD

Lewis Thomas

This book deals with the most powerful and popular communication device ever invented for spreading information and ideas around the globe: television, and with the ways it is being used for the benefit of the human beings most in need of facts and notions about the world: children.

Although the points of view are fascinatingly different, these essays represent a not surprising consensus on two counts. Almost everyone is depressed by the generally low quality of what television has accomplished so far and is dismayed by the failure of the machine, up to now, to give children a lasting interest in science. At the same time, there is near unanimity in the belief that the things that *can* be done are simply wonderful to think about. The proposals in this book vary in approach and detail, but underlying them all is a sense of exhilaration that such an educational instrument as television can be placed at the disposal of science teachers.

Whatever else is done in the future, I hope the educators and TV program writers will take pains to disconnect science from technology, and present these activities as two quite separate kinds of endeavor. I agree with those who say that the two are tightly linked in real life—one thing leading straight to another—but it seems to me that they are of educational interest and importance for quite different reasons. Moreover, different age groups perceive them differently.

It used to surprise me that young children are almost never surprised by things I would have thought they should find absolutely flabbergasting. Switching on a light bulb is taken for granted, if noticed at all. The dial telephone is used with enthusiasm by very young people, but never wondered at. An airplane is just another airplane, even when seen or traveled on for the first time. Computer games are intoxicating and addictive, but only because of the dazzlement controlled by moving human fingers. As for television itself, it is simply part of the room, more fun to look at than a blank wall but no more puzzling. I keep thinking that if I were a child I would be knocked off my feet by technology, in the same way that a word processor terrifies and magnetizes me today. For young children, however, machines are the inanimate world.

Lewis Thomas, M.D., is Chancellor of the Memorial Sloan-Kettering Cancer Center and author of many books and articles about science for the general public, including The Lives of a Cell, *which won a National Book Award.*

FOREWORD

I remember an experience some years back, on the event of the first manned moon shot. My wife and I were sitting in the stands at Cape Kennedy, surrounded by other interested parties and their children. A huge voice announced the countdown, and then the thing went off, roaring fire and thunder and lifting off on its terrifying trajectory. Exuberance and jubilation were cried aloud by all the adults. Then I noticed a small boy pointing and jumping up and down in excitement, pointing not to the monstrous vehicle but off to the side. At all edges, in a vast circle around the launch site, a great flight of marsh birds had come aloft, poised in the air for a few minutes, then fluttered down again into the reeds. "Look, look!" the child cried out at everyone.

I also remember, from even longer ago, a conference on science education held in Boston, where Professor Jerrold Zacharias had come to demonstrate a new idea he had for getting young children interested in science. It was a cardboard box, filled with mealworms. The participants in the conference were mostly scientists, tenured members of the academic establishment. They peered into Zacharias's box in puzzlement and then began poking their fingers in, asking questions and then shouting different answers at each other in rising voices—not exactly jumping up and down but coming close to it, having a marvelous time.

If you are looking for ways to catch the close attention of children—any age children—show them, for starters, a small bird or a monarch butterfly or a nest of mealworms. Things that are alive are the most wonderful mysteries. To teach science, and to want to learn science, you have to have in mind some questions beyond answering, questions that raise other questions. Once that is done, the details become more and more attractive.

Television is made for this kind of display, it seems to me, carrying the mind down to the deepest and smallest parts of nature, and out to the farthest reaches of the cosmos. But it should start with things that wiggle.

INTRODUCTION

Kim Hays

I contend that a general scientific literacy will be one of the ingredients for coping with the problems of technology. By scientific literacy I do not mean familiarity with the professional technical journals, but rather a general, nonmathematical understanding of enough of the content and method of the various sciences to match our "literacy" in other important aspects of life.

Robert R. Wilson, physicist
"The New Literature of Science"
The Bulletin of the Atomic Scientists,
April 1981

Many people today feel uncomfortable with and sometimes hostile toward scientists. That is nothing new; at least we no longer stone scientists, put them in prison, or burn them at the stake. Many school children today will graduate from high school with insufficient formal instruction in science. Yet during the past thirty years more children have received at least some formal instruction in science than ever before.

That is where the comfort of a historical perspective ends. The fact is that our current familiarity with technology has not brought us a corresponding familiarity with science, although we tend to use the two words interchangeably. Science is a body of theories (some all but indisputable, others highly hypothetical) that have grown out of a particular method of investigation. This method—observation of and experimentation with nature—is used to test the likelihood of scientists' guesses about how things work. Technology is the application of scientific theories in order to create tools. Today we think we are "scientific" because we use any tool, from a tire jack to a computer, with great confidence. But most of us have no idea of the scientific process that preceded the invention of the tool, nor of the scientific theories that explain why it works. Nor do we care.

What do most adolescents think of science (not the classroom subject, but the field as a whole)? Ask a thirteen-year-old, and he or she is likely to call science "weird." The word says more about our feelings toward science than the user may be aware of, not only in the idiomatic meaning of the word, but in its real meanings: relating to or dealing with fate or the Fates; magical, unearthly, mysterious, odd, eerie, uncanny. We perceive the sciences, with their frequent medical and military applications, to have enormous impact on our fate as individuals and as a society, yet we feel helpless to influence the products of scientific research. As a result, we treat scientists as both gods and scapegoats. "They screwed everything up and they can damn well fix it" expresses a common attitude toward scientists.

The essays in this book examine some of the causes for our feelings about science and scientists: the way science is taught in school, the way scientists are portrayed by the media. The authors also point out the economic and political dangers of our scientific illiteracy, which causes us not only to shy away from science as a career but also to refrain from thoughtful criticism of its applications. As a partial solution to these problems, the authors discuss what television can do to help children grow up feeling more comfortable with and knowledgeable about science.

Why television? Why shouldn't parents or teachers shoulder the responsibility? Why not emphasize the importance of books, newspapers, magazines, movies, and other media? The answer is that all of these other influences are important—in some cases more important than television—and many of them are discussed in this book. But television, which plays an enormously important role in the lives of American children, has a special obligation to them. Most people take television so much for granted that they forget broadcasters' enormous privilege and power: the privilege to use the public's airwaves, a limited spectrum, to make money; the power to reach millions of people instantly and tell them what to think about everything from the president's foreign policy to deodorant soap. To keep the spectrum from being overloaded with signals, broadcasters must be granted a license to operate by the Federal Communications Commission. That license obligates them to perform their job "in the public interest, convenience, and necessity." Children, who in 1983 watched an average of 26 hours of television a week, are part of that public. Yet commercial broadcasters provide little more than Saturday morning cartoons for them to watch. As a result, science is only one of the many subjects about which television either fails to inform children or else misinforms them.

Most members of the television profession, like other people, want their powers and privileges without the accompanying obligations. Or, if they are thoughtful people, they recognize their obligations but find them so vast as to defy close scrutiny. As a result, a great many of them take refuge in doing *something* "in the public interest" to salve their consciences—and meet FCC requirements—but rarely enough to make a difference.

To broadcasters, then, this book offers some suggestions about how to make a real difference in young people's attitudes toward science. And to the rest of us, the book offers a goal: to make science education a priority, on TV as well as in the classroom. When enough people want to see more and better science programming on TV, we will get it—but not before then.

SCIENCE,
and
KIDS

TEACHING OUR CHILDREN
TO QUESTION

CHALLENGING THE TELEVISION INDUSTRY

Every great advance in science has issued from a new audacity of imagination.

John Dewey, *educator and philosopher*
(1859–1952)

I f it takes imagination to be a good scientist, it also takes imagination to be a good producer of science TV programming, especially for young people. Gerald Holton, Mallinckrodt Professor of Physics and professor of the history of science at Harvard University, challenges TV producers to help the public achieve greater scientific literacy. On a similar note, producer Adrian Malone, who is responsible for "The Ascent of Man" and "Cosmos" (which became the most-watched public television series when it was first aired in 1980) writes about what he perceives to be his responsibilities as a science producer. Finally, Anne Briscoe, a biochemist, past president of the Association for Women in Science, and a faculty member of Columbia University's College of Physicians and Surgeons, examines some of the causes of the exclusion of women and minorities from scientific careers and urges producers to use television to help eliminate racism and sexism from our society.

1

THE STRUGGLE FOR SCIENTIFIC MATURITY

Gerald Holton

Can anything new and useful be said, in a few pages, to make a case—once again—for more and better science on television for children? The arguments from intellectual and social need are obvious enough, but they clearly have not swayed the decision makers in the United States. Neither children nor the sciences are causes that have enough "bottom-line" appeal for broadcasters, and putting the two together seems to make them even less appealing. Perhaps some day there will appear a combination of Savonarola and Sam Adams who is able to shame the television industry—one of the most profitable in the world in terms of the ratio of new profits to production costs—into doing what it should, but I have no illusions about my own powers of persuasion.

Nevertheless, at least for the record, let us sketch out one of the arguments in favor of science programming for young people. And while we are at it, let us choose the most ambitious one.

We now know well that the mind of a young child is (perhaps unfortunately) not a tabula rasa. On the contrary, the child has a great deal of patchy but quite functional knowledge on a vast variety of subjects. One of these subjects is how nature works—something we could consider an elementary form of science or engineering. Parents and elementary school teachers can provide a list of elements that make up a typical child's knowledge, such as:

- Material bodies come to a stop unless they are pushed.

- A fur piece keeps you warm because it once covered the warm body of an animal.

- Electricity flows through wires as water does through pipes, only much faster.

Gerald Holton, Ph.D., is Mallinckrodt Professor of Physics and professor of the history of science at Harvard University. He is a member of the National Commission on Excellence in Education and coauthor of its 1983 report, A Nation at Risk: The Imperative for Educational Reform.

3

- Evolution is a theory about animals that is still debated by academics; if it ever was true, it refers to events in the distant past.

- Space is a big container, and matter appeared in it at the beginning of time.

- Time is the same everywhere and marches on inexorably, as if to the beat of an absolute and universal clock.

In addition to these assumptions about how things work, a child's knowledge about nature includes simplistic methodological perceptions. A sampling of these, in no particular order:

- Knowing the name of a thing is a key to knowing what things "are."

- Scientists discover, whereas artists create.

- Science and engineering are hardly distinguishable.

- The sure way to knowledge is by building theories based on observation.

- The pattern of "causes and effects" works most of the time, but incomprehensible and magical things do occasionally intervene.

- Hypotheses are essentially wild guesses.

- If we are to understand how things work, we need models that are touchable or at least visualizable; and anthropomorphic conceptions are also useful.

- Scientific concepts have an independent and unchangeable existence.

- Science is truth; nevertheless, from time to time, everything known before turns out to have been entirely wrong, and a revolution is needed to establish the *real* truth.

- There is an infinite yet ever-increasing mass of scientific facts, among which there is little interconnection or interdependence.

What this amounts to is a somewhat pre-Aristotelian picture of the natural world, about which the least interesting thing to say is that it is *wrong*. Like a child's first attempt at speech, it is legitimate knowledge. This elementary sense of the natural world is functional in three ways: it organizes and explains, up to a point, what is going on; it serves as a framework for interacting with the environment; and it offers a foundation for developing a more adequate world picture.

The goal of "The Science Alliance," TVOntario's instructional series for fourth-, fifth-, and sixth-graders, is to help kids love science. *Photo courtesy of TVOntario.*

The last is the most important. Gaining scientific literacy means leaving that "baby-talk" scientific world picture behind, and advancing to the more sophisticated one. In the "grown-up" world, mankind does not have a central position, and evolution is a fact of contemporary life, applicable on many levels from biology to cosmology. In this world, absolutes have disappeared, and classical causality has been replaced by the assumption that probability—not certainty—plays a basic role. Concepts are often nonvisualizable and expressed in mathematical formulas; they are man-made and thus are always subject to change. The number and complexity of facts and details are still vast but there is a dense network of connections between them, and at the bottom there are relatively few laws—some known in great detail—that run the whole show in all its diversity.

For a young person, the labor of getting from the pre-Aristotelian to the post-Darwinian, post-Einsteinian world picture is enormous, for two reasons. First, there is the matter of the ever-increasing distance between the two

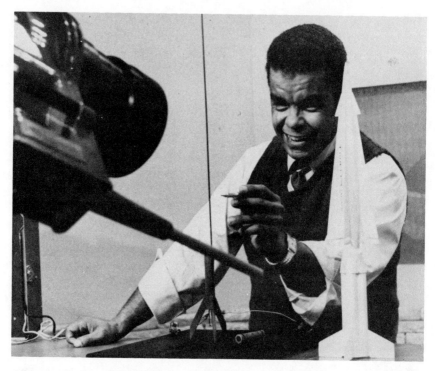

Television science teacher Robert Crumpler demonstrates rocket engine propulsion principles and rapid combustion as a power source in the "Process and Proof" science series targeted to sixth-grade students. Crumpler has hosted three other instructional science series, "Search for Science," "Tell Me What You See," and "The Science Room," all produced by WVIZ-TV, Cleveland. *Photo courtesy of Great Plains National ITV Library.*

worlds. While the distance from baby language to tolerable verbal literacy has not been all that different from century to century and can be overcome, in principle, in the first few decades of life, this is not true for the case of science, where the distance grows constantly larger as the body of scientific knowledge expands and is transformed. Worse, gaining scientific literacy is a matter not merely of evolving from primitive ideas to complex ones, but of tearing out and replacing a whole, originally functional world picture, with all its concepts, hypotheses, and metaphors. This is analogous to changing languages, not merely improving on one, and is a task so difficult that it is not fully accomplished even by many scientists, except in their own narrow fields of special expertise.

For most other people, what seems to happen is this. First, they graft onto the baby-talk scientific world picture of the "savage" mind a jumble of terms and fragments of unconnected information—from "black holes" to *Drosophila* fruit flies, from "everything is relative" to tenth-grade algebra (for most Americans today, the sorry acme and endpoint of their scientific and mathematical training). But along the way, people begin to suspect that even with their earnest efforts to respond to these new bits of information, something is fundamentally wrong—that they are still talking baby talk and are too far gone to do much better. So they become embarrassed and ashamed and turn against the effort itself. The best of them feel pain and resentment over their disconnection from one of the awesome accomplishments of our civilization, the contemporary scientific world view.

There is a second reason why the transition between the two scientific worlds is so difficult. The child who is learning to speak a more mature form of language gets a lot of help. Every step of his way, in the home and outside it, he will find adults (and perhaps other siblings) who understand "baby talk" but also already know mature language. These are people with whom the learner can constantly interact as the old language is being replaced by the new one. This is not the case for the changeover from the primitive to the new scientific world picture. Here, the child's source of help and interaction is almost always limited to the parsimonious fare of the American schoolroom, where the modern hope for "some science every day" is still a utopian dream. And the adults around the learner of science, including the parents and many of the teachers, are themselves usually still stranded at the level of the baby-talk scientific world picture.

Although television is only one science-teaching tool among many, it can be useful to the learner of science in specific ways, because of the particular strengths of video technology. Television is the ideal medium for making available the visual experience of a vast variety of scientific phenomena that are otherwise inaccessible. Because of its ability to capture motion, television can also be very good at explaining how things work and what the time scale or dimension of events is. Moreover, television can roam everywhere for its examples—to the sports field, to other continents, into the ocean, and, using telescopes and microscopes, into space or into a cell.

Television can arouse over and over again the child's natural curiosity about nature's doings. The young human mind craves information and is designed to accommodate it. Before the future expert can achieve some sophistication, he or she needs to have absorbed a large number of individual particles of knowledge that can later be assembled into the "chunks" of information that will constitute the base of expertise.[1] Of course, a TV portrayal lacks the authenticity of an actual three-dimensional event in real time.

Nothing will replace playing with a compass or planting seeds or watching a solar eclipse or the birth of kittens. Yet the ability of television to offer a wide variety of topics that will intrigue a young viewer nevertheless makes it an important aid to learning.

The TV set is available now in practically every home, all the time, and without additional direct expense. It stands ready to fulfill its civilizing function at the flick of a switch. It is unfortunate that much of what passes for science on TV today is inadequate, but the potential for creative programming is still there. Television can pool the resources and products of providers of good science programs wherever they may be. Unlike the family or the classroom teacher, television can use cable or satellite to plug into a universe of science programming, from San Francisco or Montreal or Tokyo. Finally, television is the only realistic way to give the great mass of people—children and adults—access to those few scientifically knowledgeable people who have the necessary skill, understanding, and dedication to help move the mind from the primitive to the more mature world picture of science.

In the process of a person's scientific maturing, the essential step of interaction must still be provided through personal contact between learners and well-trained teachers, in the classroom or at home. But TV programming specifically developed to assist in this process would be invaluable. What stands in the way of such programming is not a lack of scientific educators who could serve as presenters, but the lack of an incentive to create programs that would use their talents. What stands in the way of better TV programming about science is that, while such programs might upgrade the level of our civilization, they won't make nearly as much money as, say, the screening of another spectacle of mayhem. Of course, this can change. But not until parents and broadcasters come to care more about the quality of our society than they do about gore and gold.

NOTE

1. Herbert A. Simon, *The Sciences of the Artificial*, 2nd ed. (Cambridge: MIT Press, 1981).

THE URGE TO UNDERSTAND

Adrian Malone

"Man is DNA's experiment in extraterrestrial life."

That observation was made to me a few years ago by Sol Spiegelman, the noted biologist. If one believes that all species inhabit a well-defined ecological niche and play an important role in evolution, one can imagine a system in which each species has a particular task. For example, whales might be historians of the seas, maintaining—like the Celts—a detailed and exact oral record in their long, idyllic songs. The dolphins, on the other hand, might be the tricksters and playboys of the animal world, living—like the hedonists—for the moment's pure pleasure. Humans' evolutionary role, suggests Spiegelman, may be as explorers in space, settlers on new planets, eventually as extraterrestrial life.

Dr. Spiegelman might be right about us, but we are not out there in space yet. Until we begin to colonize other planets, we remain residents of a fourth-rate planet orbiting a third-rate sun—and we wait, sometimes impatiently, to gather enough strength and wisdom to take the next major step in man's evolution.

We have, in our heads, a powerful engine of exploration that needs to be constantly exercised. That exercise takes many forms. We create from our imagination any number of scenarios about our past, our present, and our future. We design and construct buildings in which to live and work—invariably square structures when there is nothing square in nature. We are continuously changing and reshaping our environment, always seeking, or so it seems, a "better" life. Sometimes we achieve elegance, sometimes disaster. While the rest of the evolutionary process, from the formation of new strains of bacteria to the adaptation of butterflies, proceeds in an orderly, Darwinian manner, we spend the whole of our existence building and rebuilding the world around us into approximations of what is inside our heads. We literally remodel the world in a Herculean attempt to explain the structures, thoughts, and mechanisms of our brains. In so doing, we discover patterns and secrets

Adrian Malone is president and executive producer of Adrian Malone Productions. He was executive producer and cowriter of "Cosmos" and, as senior producer at the BBC, he produced "The Ascent of Man." He is currently working on several projects with Embassy Television.

Scientist and philosopher Jacob Bronowski hosted "The Ascent of Man," the BBC/ Time-Life series about the growth of man's knowledge, produced by Adrian Malone. *Photo courtesy of WGBH, Boston.*

that nature has already struggled for eons to perfect. This is good, since each new discovery is in keeping with our evolutionary role of explorer. Unfortunately, however, we also tamper with nature's patterns—sometimes indiscriminately—without knowing the whole context in which nature operates. This is bad, since it often results in the destruction of nature's balance. When we humans try to achieve "progress" by leaping over the time needed for adaptation to occur naturally, we can turn a process of slow change into a wrenching explosion. If we are to be evolution's research laboratory, we must exercise greater care and patience with our environment. Our responsibility to planet Earth is too great to do otherwise.

Before the scientific revolution began, the force that bound most men and women was religion, a belief in God that demanded an act of faith. Then the pendulum swung heavily in the other direction, toward science, an investigative method that insisted upon proof. Now I believe it is beginning to swing back toward the middle as we come to understand that science is really just another word for knowledge. There appears to be a growing recognition by learned men and women that there must be a synthesis, an understanding of all of the parts that make up the whole. That synthesis is what I strive to achieve in every television series I produce.

If television is only a window, if it is only a peep show, if it is only a moving panel in the wall, then let us only read books. But if television is used to tell a story that excites our imagination, stimulates our intellect, and moves us to laugh or cry, then it deserves a place in our lives.

Television can bring together science and art, humor and pathos, and the countless lineaments of understanding into a single experience. Too often, however, science programs are stereotypical; that is, their information is presented in a rigidly linear fashion with little or no attempt made to connect that particular aspect of scientific inquiry with any other aspect of our lives. But if sound and visuals are used imaginatively, television can portray recognizable patterns, some linear and others woven in and out like a recurring theme from a musical score. The difficulty is to create a pattern that can be understood by the widest possible audience without reverting to stereotypes.

Too often, children's programming, especially Saturday morning cartoons, depends heavily on stereotyping. The characters are either "good" or "evil"; children are either smart or dumb; parents are either a help or a hindrance; animals are either loved or feared. As a result, characters are shallow and their behavior is inevitably predictable. It is the easy way out for the storyteller.

To make connections that have not been made before: this is exciting television. To find the connecting link between seemingly disparate pieces of information and then to design the visual and audible connection that makes it work for the audience is what I believe sets quality programming apart from that which is commonplace. It is a difficult challenge. In order to make connections which are unique, it is critical that one have an understanding of human variance. That understanding can only come with an education that includes all aspects of man's knowledge, scientific and humanistic.

At the beginning of his life, a young Tuscan, Leonardo da Vinci, wrote over and over a single sentence, "I wish to work miracles." At the end of his life he repeatedly wrote, "Tell me if anything ever was done." Although he is perceived as a genius, Leonardo da Vinci judged himself a failure. Despite his extraordinary achievements, da Vinci never stopped searching and wondering.

He spanned the gamut of specialties from engineer to sculptor, from artist to scientist. For me, his life is an object lesson, because he tried to understand the process of all things and was not satisfied only to possess the artifact. In all the generations following him, there have been people who believed that his search is the human birthright and duty.

To understand the spectrum of nature and man's place in it is a goal fit for a whole lifetime. We have discrete ways of understanding: books, talk, experience, work, education, the example of parents and teachers. And we have television. No television producer is Leonardo da Vinci, and no box filled with images on a screen is *The Virgin of the Rocks*. But, if a television series tells me something new about my humanity in the context of physics, chemistry, or biology, then it is good. If it also surprises, inspires, educates, and entertains me, then it is very good. If, however, it goes that extra step and cracks open the mind with a blinding light, then it is excellent.

DESEGREGATING SCIENCE

Anne M. Briscoe

How can television be used to excite the young imagination, to inspire children—girls and boys, racial and ethnic minorities—with a dream that will lead many of them to seek careers in the wide world of science and technology?

Here we are in the midst of an incredible computer revolution more profound than the impact of the printing press or the replacement of handmade by machine-made goods. We are threatened with extinction in a nuclear holocaust. The "man in the moon" has become men on the moon and the "green cheese" turned into rocks brought back to earth. At the same time, women and minorities are challenging the major premise of society: white male dominance. The essence of our era is swift, profound change—technological and philosophical—that demands, but does not yet have, equally rapid change in the educational system to prepare young minds and hearts for this brave new world.

Our nation faces a major crisis in science education, resulting in part from a shortage of teachers in mathematics and the sciences that is due to several factors: low salaries for teachers relative to those earned by workers in industry; low prestige; and low job satisfaction in the teaching field. There is a dangerous shortfall in the supply of scientists and engineers for the industrial, strategic, and educational needs of our country. Yet despite the need to develop our human resources to the fullest, patterns of institutional racism and sexism pervade our social order and obliterate in childhood the potential talent of more than half the population. Only eighteen percent of men in college major in science or engineering. Even worse, out of young women, who comprise over fifty percent of the college population, only seven percent choose science or engineering as a major.[1]

Without a new set of values, we cannot alter the patterns of segregation and discrimination in the workplace. And the workplace simply mirrors the home, school, church—in short, the whole of society—in exploitation of minorities and discrimination against women. In examining the fields that have not attracted women or minorities in significant numbers, one finds engineer-

Anne M. Briscoe, Ph.D., *is a member of the faculty of Columbia University's College of Physicians and Surgeons at Harlem Hospital Center, where she is a clinical laboratory director. She is also a past president of the Association for Women in Science.*

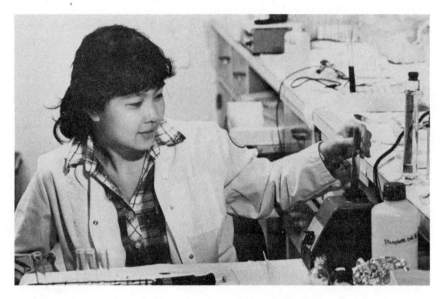

Seventeen-year-old Jeanne Lo is one of the young scientists featured in "Spaces," a six-part public television series that highlights the achievements of black, Hispanic, Asian, and Native American scientists. "Spaces" is a production of WETA-Washington, D.C., in association with InterAmerica Research Associates. *Photo by Joseph Schuyler.*

ing, physics, astronomy, geology, and mathematics. Instead, women choose to pursue psychology, anthropology, sociology, and the humanities—the fields with fewer job opportunities and lower salaries. They do this in part because they have been socialized to believe that they lack the innate ability to succeed in "hard" sciences and math, and in part because of the outright discrimination they have encountered in the fields men have tried to preserve for themselves alone. For instance, data collected by the American Chemical Society on the appointment of women to faculty positions show that nearly half of the U.S. research universities, all of which grant Ph.D.s to women every year, have never had a woman at faculty rank in the chemistry department.

Because television plays a major national role in the communication of ideas, it has an incalculable influence on American life. With a commitment to the principles of equality, the industry could make a long-range, centralized effort to change the next generation. One must consider the slow pace of enlightenment. It has been one hundred years since Darwin died, a quarter of a century since we began carbon-dating rocks and fossils, over a decade since the moon landing. Yet a significant segment of society believes that the Bible is the authoritative source of knowledge about the earth, the universe, and human history. "Creation science" may have lost a court battle, but it has a huge following. In fact, the Equal Rights Amendment—a significant step in the direction of equality—was defeated partly because of the power of religious teachings like creation science. For many women, as for men, the belief in woman as an extension of man—Adam's rib, created only for his benefit—justifies the inferior position women occupy. We must attack this doctrine head-on.

Unfortunately, if television were to offer an accurate portrayal of what lies ahead for girls and minority children who are interested in the sciences, young people might give up before they started. They would perceive that the prospects for a successful career in the sciences remain remote. They might decide that the odds of becoming a successful scientist are poorer than the odds of becoming a rock star, world tennis champ, TV newscaster, or major league professional baseball player. If there is to be a change in these children's prospects for a science career, parents, teachers, employers, and the scientific establishment must be persuaded that the talent of more than half the world is underdeveloped and that industry, the Gross National Product, and our economy would all be better served by the full development of all our resources.

Perhaps what we should do is not try to deny the problem, but instead dramatize the genius that women and minorities have been able to show in special circumstances. For example, the twelve greatest women mathematicians who were given a place in history by feminist scholar Teri Perl were nearly all daughters of wealthy, educated, and socially powerful men.[2] Only one of these women is given even a brief mention in the four-volume tome by James R. Newman, *The World of Mathematics.* The stories of other women and minorities whose discoveries and accomplishments have been overlooked, minimized, or credited to a white man deserve attention. For instance, Daniel Hale Williams, a black doctor at the Provident Hospital in Chicago, was the first to operate successfully on the human heart in 1893, although this singular contribution to medicine has not always been recognized.

Above all, there is one important science history film shown repeatedly on television that I yearn to see replaced with a new and correct version. This is the "NOVA" film purporting to present the story of the discovery of the structure of DNA by James D. Watson. To set the record straight, the late Dr. Rosalind Franklin must be given her place of distinction for providing the essential X-ray diffraction evidence of the double helical structure. Like Watson's book, *The Double Helix,* which is on reading lists at many high schools, the "NOVA" film denigrates Franklin's scientific competence as well as her person. The true story was published in a 1975 book by Anne Sayre called *Rosalind Franklin and DNA.*[3] A film version based on Sayre's carefully researched and documented biography would illustrate the techniques used by some men (fortunately not all) to defame their female competitors and rob them of respect as well as credit for their accomplishments. Such a revised film would speak not only for Franklin but for all women who have had to fight for recognition that is rightfully theirs. Equally important, it would give young people a role model they could rightfully aspire to. Of course, it would also warn them of the obstacles facing them, but an exciting TV drama, with a great actress playing Rosalind Franklin, might inspire them to confront the prejudices that stand in their way.

Television must undertake the mission of awakening the conscience and the consciousness of both young and old. Unenlightened adults who believe in white male superiority are an obstacle to progress because they transmit their prejudices to their children. Women, having been victims of and believers in their own inferiority, often perpetuate the myth of male superiority. Eleanor Roosevelt said that no one can make you feel inferior without your consent. Women must learn not to consent.

A college dean once told me that he could create or eliminate a college tradition in four years; four years is a generation in college time. Television theoretically needs twenty years to train a new generation, but I suspect that the time frame could be greatly reduced.

Come on, broadcasters! You and your friends on Madison Avenue know the most sophisticated methods of mind manipulation. Use them. Persuade. Command. Hypnotize. Try the soft sell. Mix it with the hard sell. Repeat daily. And then practice what you preach: hire and promote more women and minorities.

NOTES

1. For specific information, it might be useful to consult Anne M. Briscoe and Sheila M. Pfafflin, eds., "Expanding the Role of Women in the Sciences," *Annals of the New York Academy of Sciences* 323 (1979). More recent information is available in the *Congressional Record* of 15 April 1982, which records testimony dealing with the importance of funds for science education as part of the budget for the National Science Foundation. This testimony was given to the U.S. Senate Committee on Labor and Human Relations. Among those testifying were: Dr. F. James Rutherford, former head of the Science Education Directorate for the National Science Foundation and current director of education at the American Association for the Advancement of Science (AAAS); Sarah E. Klein, president of the National Science Teachers Association; Dr. Lewis Salter, president of Wabash College; John E. Gibson, dean of engineering at the University of Virginia; and myself, representing the Association for Women in Science, the Woman Scientists' Committee of the New York Academy of Sciences, and the New York City Commission on the Status of Women.

2. Teri Perl, *Math Equals: Biographies of Women Mathematicians* (Reading, Mass.: Addison-Wesley, 1978). Other books that offer stories of women scientists that could be televised are Louis Haber's *Women Pioneers of Science*, rev. ed. (New York: Harcourt Brace Jovanovich, 1979) and Iris Noble's *Contemporary Women Scientists of America* (New York: Julian Messner, 1979).

3. Anne Sayre, *Rosalind Franklin and DNA* (New York: W. W. Norton, 1975).

SCIENCE ON THE SET

Science commits suicide when it adopts a creed.

Thomas Henry Huxley, biologist (1825–1895)

Children's images of science and their positive or negative feelings about it as a subject of study and a career path are forged from miscellaneous bits of information from many sources. Television is only one of these sources, but it is an important one. There is no single "truth" about science that television should be communicating to children. Instead, the authors of the essays in this chapter suggest a variety of ways in which television should, and should not, portray science and scientists, if it is to make science more accessible to young people.

Bradley Greenberg, chairman of the Department of Communication at Michigan State University and an expert at content analyses of television, has taken a critical look at the messages about science communicated by Saturday morning TV cartoons. Cary Lu, a biologist who has worked on several science TV shows and is now executive editor of *High Technology*, takes a more general look at television content and argues for accurate portrayals of science in everything from the news to prime-time drama.

The feasibility of successful science programming is illustrated in an interview with Don Herbert, better known as Mr. Wizard to those who watched his long-running NBC series or have seen his new programs on Nickelodeon. In the next essay, MIT physics professor Philip Morrison and Phylis Morrison, a writer and teacher, draw on their combined experience with science, education, and television production to offer the television industry specific suggestions about how to enliven science presentations.

Josephine Gladstone, a children's writer and a producer of science television, has used recollections of her own childhood to show the role television can play in stimulating young people's curiosity and enthusiasm about science. Fred Jerome, director of the Media Resources Service at the Scientists' Institute for Public Information, closes this chapter by imagining the kind of science series a twelve-year-old would like to see on TV.

17

SATURDAY MORNING SCIENCE

Bradley S. Greenberg

The words "science" or "scientist" may be heard only two or three times during a typical Saturday morning of network television. But those direct references do not represent a fraction of the content that is likely to influence a young viewer's conception of what science is all about. Saturday morning programming yields a wholesale garbling of scientific gadgetry and magical powers, mixing the plausible with the impossible, mortality with invulnerability, and altruism with aggression.

Asked to describe the manner in which science is portrayed on television and to posit the impact of that content on children, I videotaped a Saturday morning on the three commercial networks and read the sparse literature on science and television.

Prior research by George Gerbner and his colleagues embeds Saturday morning TV in the context of all television.[1] They systematically analyzed fictional programs from 1973 to 1979 and found that six out of ten prime-time and seven out of ten weekend daytime shows involved themes "explicitly and unambiguously related to science, technology, or engineering." They found science to be the central focus of four percent of prime-time and nine percent of weekend daytime shows. Scientific content was associated with violent content; both occurred more often together than separately. About one-third of science-related shows were set in strange space or time locations, emphasizing the "exotic and dangerous aspects of the dramatic image of science." Scientists were infrequently portrayed; as a career, science represented less than one percent of the prime-time occupations observed. On weekend children's shows, scientists were judged "less rational and stable and much more violent than other characters."

My own immersion in a single morning of television yielded such vivid impressions about science-related issues that I think a recitation of the major scientific themes is particularly enlightening and, perhaps, disconcerting.

The predominant representation of science on Saturday morning TV is through science's output, its products: gadgetry, machines, devices, and inven-

Bradley S. Greenberg, *Ph.D., is chairman of the department of communication at Michigan State University and author of* Life on Television *and* Mexican Americans and the Mass Media.

Saturday morning bright spots, the "Science Rock" messages are produced for Scholastic Rock by Newall and Yohe, Inc., and appear on the ABC Television Network. This one, about Isaac Newton, is called "A Victim of Gravity." © *American Broadcasting Company.*

tions that can do anything conceivable and then some. How these inventions got there, how they were made, and who helped make them are not fodder for Saturday morning shows. In general, the gadgets are shown and used as if they were as common as forks. Many of these high-tech products are clearly linked to space-age technology that youngsters are likely to have seen or read something about. Computers match dance partners and control rockets. Jets attached to shoes save our heroes, and an X-ray bracelet comes in handy. Robots clean house, stand guard, serve as pets, and make wishes come true. Space ships take us everywhere—to Mars and Venus, backwards in time, forward to alien planets. Electromagnets steal secrets; voice-activated devices open a safe in a swimming pool.

The cartoons create enough familiarity with these gadgets to blur what is from what may be someday. And that's okay. It gives youngsters expectations of what may result from continuing efforts to invent new tools, and it stimulates imagination. The diversity and creativity of the abundant high-tech devices on these shows may convey the programs' most positive message about science.

At the same time, the gadgetry creates a single-minded focus on technology rather than science, on things that go "whiz-bang," on instantaneous solutions to crises and threats. The avid viewer of Saturday morning on all three networks is likely to emerge with no conception of science apart from technology, and no sense of the scientific process.

A very large share of the technological devices function as weaponry. These products of science are directed against other people or creatures and eventually turn on their evil creators. Missiles, rockets, man-made volcanoes and avalanches, electrical shocks, and laser beams are only a few examples. These relatively sophisticated weapons are supplemented by the arsenals of more primitive weapons that are part of a typical Saturday morning. Serving a variety of destructive functions on the morning I viewed programs were:

spears	bows and arrows
catapults	hand grenades
swords	dynamite
cannons	sledgehammers
pistols	animal traps
mallets	rock crushers
spades and picks	glue
land mines	gas
trucks	farm implements
knives	rocks

The partnership between science and violence is cemented by the sheer magnitude of the destructive intentions this list of weapons illustrates. To the extent that a young viewer obtains from television notions about technology, science, and their roles in society, he or she is more likely to come away believing in their life-threatening, rather than life-enhancing, functions.

Intertwined with this display of destruction is the notion of the invulnerability of the cartoon character, whether human, alien, or otherwise anthropomorphic. We understand the special gifts of the superhero: he has been endowed with strengths that defy real harm, although even he experiences some short-term setbacks while subduing villains whose strength is temporarily equal to his own. But those who appear to be mortal are equally immune to harm from any source. The only lasting damage that occurs is to the machinery—robots are dismantled, computers go askew. The consequence of violence is never lasting physical harm to an animate object, even a villain. On Saturday morning, no one bleeds, dies, or suffers for long. This format is repeated throughout the morning. For younger viewers, this singular emphasis on violence as humor, on the ability of the body to withstand such onslaughts, on what can be termed "clean violence," is a distortion of both science and our sensibilities.

Another theme found in tandem with scientific gadgets is the debunking of them. This takes two forms. First, gadgets don't work right. The weaponry is inept; it only confuses, delays, de-furs, defrocks, or angers its wielders. The people processor won't start until the young heroine kicks it; Fonzie's time machine is waterlogged by its own fire extinguishers; a computer goes berserk and is seemingly permanently unplugged.

The second form of scientific product debunking is that it takes little if any special skill to operate or to thwart the gadgets, to "do" science. Here's an example from one program, during a computer-dating episode. The arrogant computer expert declares, "Never underestimate the importance of the computer to help man do his thinking. . . . The computer is always right. . . . The computer replaces man." The schoolkids easily reprogram the computer by punching an assortment of buttons, discuss how they will falsify data, and then drop the new data cards into a large slot in the machine, which goes haywire. Obviously a victory for children over authority.

On this particular Saturday morning, two cartoons involved lead characters inadvertently trapped in space vehicles. Laverne and Shirley accidentally launch themselves in a space rocket, but on-the-job practice quickly puts them in command of the vehicle. It "doesn't run on pedals and rubber bands, it runs on gizmos and whatchamacallits," says one of the heroines. Scooby Doo and his friends also blast off from a space center. Within seconds, both gravity and meteor showers are discussed and comically and erroneously demonstrated. In about the same amount of time, the stowaways take the command of the ship away from the control center, rebuild the mission's robot into a toy Mars-mobile, and then rebuild it again into a robot that exhorts "robot power." Optimists may suggest that such portrayals demystify technology rather than debunk it. But there is no how-to information; inspired dumb luck resolves problem situations that involve heroes and heroines. The right buttons are there and random punching will do it.

When villains make elaborate efforts to use technology as weaponry—in order to take over the world or eat their victims or whatever—the hero steps in with ingenuity and luck to quickly turn technology against the aggressor. Not only does the coyote get crushed in his rock-crusher, but Illuso is zapped with his own laser wand, and the evil Venusian spaceship is reprogrammed to send it hurtling out of control through the solar system—all by heroes whose split-second learning and responses are error-proof.

There is on Saturday morning a particular fascination with a class of inventions that transform things and, even more often, transform people. On this one Saturday, I watched a machine process people into green, part-alligator "Hissmen," a laser wand change people into Zombies, special machines duplicate people, a glowing medallion turn people into stone, another medallion turn people into werewolves, and time tubes and time machines move people through eons. In addition, there were transporters that moved people through space, levitators that raised them, and miniaturization devices that shrank them. These transformation devices were accompanied by the more traditional transformations of mortals into their super selves by the incantation of magic words or the donning of special garb. It is as if the primary mission of science, or at least of inventors, were to provide the possibility of wholesale change of ourselves. This feeds a child's wish to be other than he is, but it also feeds his apprehension about who has the power to change him. Certainly, television seems to say, it is not safe for scientists to have that power. (In real life, much of science *is* focused on implementing changes in humans, but on a more specific basis and generally for altruistic, not evil, purposes.)

How are scientists portrayed? Those identified as scientists or technicians or professors, placed in laboratories and white coats, would be called stupid or silly by youngsters. They may be technical geniuses, but they have no control over what they're doing. They are all inept at dealing with the problems they create. On one program, a scientist who harnesses geysers as an energy source is unaware that his discovery is being used by his boss to flood the trails used by pioneer wagon trains. A computer programmer matching dancing partners is befuddled by false information dropped into the machine and subsequently dismisses the computer as useless when the matches are inappropriate. A white-coated professor in his laboratory cannot remember the magic words that will turn his carpet into a rocket ship. He uses the wrong words; it rolls up around him and drops him out the window. Two space center scientists cannot figure out how Scooby and his friends got to Mars. And these are the "good" scientists!

The "hero" scientists did not exist. No bright and cheerful man or woman was depicted as doing anything that could be remotely considered improving the lot of the human race through invention, discovery, or research—at least, not successfully. The bad scientists are a little more competent, but ultimately they, too, fail. The moral of each story is that the evildoer will be foiled, that crime does not pay. But there is no extension of the moral to include the concept that what was used for evil could otherwise be used for good, that identifying new energy sources, for example, or harnessing existing ones like water power could be beneficial. The concluding scene of each story shows the happiness of the victor and the dismay of the villain; science and technology have no lasting place.

Interludes in this morning of technological violence and transformation consisted of commercials and some few, but significant, public service announcements (PSAs). Commercials pushing toys and food were repeated throughout the morning and across the different networks (some I saw five or six times). The transitions to the PSAs were abrupt. These messages, so different in format and content from the materials surrounding them, were often about science. Suddenly, we learned about the composition of air, how crayons work, how to give artificial respiration, the importance of eating breakfast, the nutritional value of potato skins, and the need for meat, eggs, and fish in your diet. There was perhaps one of these PSAs per hour on each network, each packing as much information as possible into thirty or sixty seconds. These messages signaled a call back to reality; they said, Think about something less fantastic for a moment. The mode of presentation was very active—bouncy music, cartoon characters, men dressed in superhero costumes—but the tone was distinctly different. It had "message" written all over it. Are these messages retained to some extent by young viewers? How do the nutrition PSAs fare in comparison to the food commercials? Is this PSA time used by children to unwind from the previous show or to wind up for the next one?

On balance, science on Saturday morning commercial network programming is an ambiguous blend of science for good and (mostly) not-so-good. The inept science worker or technician; the consistently clever, creative, and technologically sophisticated villain upended by the hero's wits or greater superpowers; and the failure of technology, or the hero's simplistic mastery of it, are prime lessons. Science, it seems to me, emerges as threatening. It is certainly not something I would want to grow up and do, if Saturday morning were my sole source of information. Luckily, it isn't. But it certainly has more pizzazz than the average fourth-grade science class. In thinking about children's learning patterns, we must ask ourselves whether a sheer quantity of images, however brief and incomplete, may have the same impact as—or greater impact than—fewer, more intense, more carefully crafted messages.

The effects of the sheer repetition of like images on the youngest and most malleable minds should not be underestimated. We should therefore expect youngsters who regularly watch cartoons to be ambivalent about the products and purposes of science and less than enthusiastic about the profession.

NOTE

1. George Gerbner, Larry Gross, Michael Morgan, and Nancy Signorielli, "Scientists on the TV Screen," *Society* 18 (1981): 41–44.

SCIENTISTS BEHIND THE SCENES

Cary Lu

Why should science be realistic on television? Is anything realistic on television?

In an earlier era, cardboard characters with cardboard emotions played out situations with no more realism than a laugh track. But the best television programs, especially today, hold their audience with believable people and stories. If an actor playing a trucker said he was putting the standard transmission into park, the show's credibility would die as every viewer who had ever driven a truck collapsed in laughter. Producers and writers who take pride in their work seek realistic portrayals, whether of trucking, banking, or science.

Realism isn't the only issue. The producer of a medical show once wanted his doctor character to give an injection to a young girl suffering from the effects of an unknown toxic substance and say, "This will take away the pain." The technical advisor protested that the scene was false and misleading; a doctor must diagnose the cause of an illness before a suitable treatment can be given. The advisor felt that the program should not lead the audience to expect unrealistic results from a magical painkiller. The producer's response was to fire the advisor for meddling. But the show's star and other executives decided that responsibility to viewers came ahead of melodrama, and so fired the producer and rehired the advisor. The show? "Quincy."

The clash between television and scientists is not surprising. The scientist, trained in precise and comprehensive explanations, mistrusts the media, regarding it as careless and imprecise. The producer, concerned about clear story lines, production values, and an inevitably tight schedule, often considers seeking expert advice an invitation to trouble.

Careers in television could not differ more from those in academia. A young scientist seeking lifelong university tenure knows that consulting for the media will not improve his or her chances of getting tenure; rather, it diverts time from projects likely to improve those chances. The established scientist often finds the brashness and compromise of television overwhelm-

Cary Lu, Ph.D., is a biologist who is executive editor of High Technology. *He has been a science advisor to Children's Television Workshop and a staff member of "NOVA."*

NBC's "Quincy M.E.," a dramatic series about a medical examiner for the Los Angeles coroner's office, won praise for its scientific accuracy. Jack Klugman played the title role. *Photo courtesy of MCA Publishing, a Division of MCA Communications, Inc. Copyright © by Universal City Studios, Inc.*

ing. Television as a medium for understanding science or scientists—either directly (as in a science show) or peripherally (as with a scientist character in a dramatic program)—is not taken seriously, much less appreciated.

But recent hard times in academia have forced many younger scientists off the tenure track to seek other ways to use their training. A few have turned to media, mainly writing; a smaller number are looking toward film and television. Unfortunately, most of them do not have sufficient basic skills for normal production positions, making it hard to justify their full-time inclusion on production teams. Only a very few scientists have actually learned film and television production and are as much at home with the media as with science.

Mark Taylor, the "Quincy" advisor who was fired and then rehired, worked for five years as a research scientist in the Los Angeles County Coroner's office before joining the production group. A coproducer of "Quincy," Taylor was also a full-time technical advisor on an entertainment program, an extremely rare phenomenon. Although the success of "Quincy" cannot be attributed to any single factor, its widely admired realism certainly played an important role. Forensic pathologist Victor Rosen reviewed every "Quincy" script with Taylor before production. Together they often added new elements and dramatic twists that enhanced both realism and drama. Taking participation even further, Taylor wrote several of the "Quincy" shows and even acted in them, because he understood how to handle the laboratory instruments featured on screen. Now, other programs are calling on Taylor. He, in turn, calls on many experts in medicine, science, and engineering to meet the needs of prospective producers.

For many shows, there is no need for a full-time science advisor. But for any science-related program, a scientist should check the concept, review the script, and occasionally work with the set designer or oversee a laboratory scene. The small cost and time investment by the program's producers will bring a crucial measure of realism and credibility. Television has a social responsibility to be realistic; programs that use the world as a stage should represent it fairly. Scientific accuracy or any other form of accuracy is no less essential than good lighting, and it's usually much cheaper.

For the past decade, the only regular television series about science has been PBS's "NOVA." Scientists have not usually served on staff (the production group is made up mostly of journalists), but the program takes scientific accuracy seriously. Scientists may help plan a show or, more often, check scripts. Frequently these scientists appear in the program. Children's Television Workshop's science series "3-2-1 Contact" was unusual for having full-time scientists on the staff who worked on every aspect of the show and were a continuous presence in the studio during taping. The scientists had veto power over anything scientific. But they never had to use it; everyone was committed to making the best possible program.

The BBC has had a long tradition of science programming through the "Horizon" series, the precursor of "NOVA." Again, scientists are not systematically involved, although an occasional staff member has been scientifically trained. Two major BBC projects sharply illustrate the advantage of a knowledgeable production staff: "The Ascent of Man" and "Connections." Jacob Bronowski, the central figure in "The Ascent of Man," had a comprehensive, if occasionally quirky, understanding of his subject. As a result, "Ascent" was frequently absorbing, insightful, and intelligent. On the other hand, neither

James Burke nor his staff on "Connections" knew enough about technology; despite impressive production values, "Connections" was spurious, with little insight or coherence. Burke was confused and the show was confused—and most of the time the audience was just as lost as Burke.

To extract the most important science features for the brief air time available calls for great expertise. The problems of clarity and accuracy are especially acute on news programs. News directors usually spurn specialists, preferring to hire generalists because they can be used interchangeably to cover a wider variety of stories. The generalist reporters argue that if they can understand a subject, they can explain it to the public. But all too often, they don't fully understand; the result is *sloppy reporting and misleading explanations.

A common example of these problems are news reports on the risks of cancer and other diseases. The evidence for these risks is fundamentally statistical, but few journalists understand the complexities of these studies, and so they confuse the public. (To be fair, some scientists who are not above grinding their own axes contribute to the confusion.) The controversy over the Love Canal chemical waste dump in Niagara Falls, for example, was widely reported as a life-threatening fiasco, yet many media reports offered little scientific evidence of significant health problems among the nearby residents. The emotional and sensationalist reporting may have served an important function by bringing the whole problem of toxic waste disposal to the nation's attention, but it did not supply the information needed to help the public understand the potential health hazards of chemical wastes. Television must help us to distinguish the truly dangerous from the merely unpleasant.

This leads to the most compelling reason for the accurate presentation of science: to make intelligent decisions in a democracy, we must understand the issues. Television, as a public medium, must face its responsibility to help us understand.

AN INTERVIEW WITH MR. WIZARD

Action for Children's Television

In May 1983, ACT interviewed Don Herbert, TV's Mr. Wizard since 1951. He and his wife Norma Herbert were just finishing production of "Mr. Wizard's World," a new show scheduled for distribution on Nickelodeon that fall. Herbert compared the 26-part cable series to his long-running NBC series and talked about his thirty-two years as TV's preeminent science teacher.

ACT: Can you compare the format of the old "Mr. Wizard" show with your new series, "Mr. Wizard's World"?

Herbert: The new series follows a magazine format, so in that sense it's very different from the old "Mr. Wizard." But the most important segments in "Mr. Wizard's World" are still the ones involving me and a child investigating some aspect of science together—the old Mr. Wizard format. I pose a problem or puzzle to the child and then we solve it together and, in the process, learn something about science or technology. That was the format for *all* of the old "Mr. Wizard" show, and it makes up about half of the segments on the new show. The other half of "Mr. Wizard's World" is different. There's the "Quick Quiz," where we ask the audience a "true or false" question like, 'Is a snowflake a drop of water frozen into a crystal?' While everyone is thinking we show them some crystal forms of water. Only twenty or thirty seconds later, we tell them the answer: FALSE, because although a snowflake *is* frozen water, it's made up of many crystals.

Then we have some "Close-up" quizzes, where we show the audience a very tight close-up of a common object and pull back slowly to reveal what it is. In one segment, we do that with a strawberry and then show some time-lapse shots of a strawberry flower maturing into the bright red berry. In another segment, a child and I do an "Everyday Magic" trick; we demonstrate the trick and then we talk about the science that makes it possible. Two longer sections don't have children in them. One is called "Safari" and is a trip to see some aspect of science or technology, and the other is called "Frontier,"

Don Herbert is the Mr. Wizard of NBC's children's television series about science (1951 to 1965) and of "Mr. Wizard's World," a science series on the children's cable channel Nickelodeon. He has also produced a series of eighty-second science news inserts for adults called "How About."

Television scientist Mr. Wizard (Don Herbert) has been doing on-camera experiments with young people for more than thirty years, first in NBC's long-running series, "Watch Mr. Wizard," and, more recently, in Nickelodeon's "Mr. Wizard's World." *Photo courtesy of Mr. Wizard Studio.*

where we show and discuss something on the frontier of knowledge—a piece of scientific equipment that's brand new or a problem that hasn't been solved yet. And then of course there are the "Spectaculars"—some of those date back to the old "Mr. Wizard" program—where we set something on fire and put it out with a fire extinguisher or blow up a can of gasoline. We do those with the children at the end of the show; they provide a good finish!

That's "Mr. Wizard's World." Comparing it to the old show is like describing the history of television. You have to remember that when we did the old program in the fifties and early sixties television was relatively new, and anything that moved or talked was fascinating. Each of our shows in those days was shaped around a single theme: friction or water vapor or something like that. We did a whole series of experiments and demonstrations and puzzles on each program that all tied in with our theme for the day. But remember that it had to be done live, in real time. So by modern standards it was very slow moving—lots of crossing back and forth and putting away and picking up and taking out equipment. And it had no visual imagination about it at all—just straight cutting with no fooling around. So you simply couldn't get as much information into a single show. On the old program, that "true or false" question about the snowflake would have been part of a whole program on snow or on water, and we'd have spent most of the half hour building up to the answer. Now, we communicate the same information, with the same impact, in a few seconds.

ACT: With all your experience as Mr. Wizard, what have you found to be the key factors in helping people enjoy science?

Herbert: When you want to explain a difficult scientific concept, the first thing you have to do is decide what specific idea you are going to talk about. You have to pick your topic very carefully. If it's too esoteric, you'll find that no one is interested in it. And if it takes too much time to explain, your audience will fade out. So, with our "How About" series of news inserts for adults, we try to ask short, to-the-point questions.

The second step is problem solving. After you've chosen your subject, pose it into a problem or a puzzle. On the "How About" series, we wanted to talk about a scientist who has developed a technique for detecting a single atom. Now, most people's response to a program on that subject would be, "So what if you can detect a single atom? I don't need to know anything about that." But if you pose the challenge as a puzzle and then give the answer as quickly and as graphically as possible, most people will stay and listen to what you have to say about the single atom. And, hopefully, they'll be intrigued.

Finally, the third step in the process of explaining scientific concepts is to be as creative as you can in presenting the solution. For example, when we were trying to show the problem of detecting a single atom, we wanted to find a way to explain to the audience the relative numbers involved. We poured a pound of salt into a dish and added one grain of sugar and asked the audience, "Could you find the grain of sugar?" Then we told them that if you had to find one grain of sugar in a million carloads of salt, *that* would be like trying to find a single atom; the order of magnitude is about the same.

That's how I try to make people more comfortable with science: by picking a simple topic, posing an interesting puzzle, and coming up with an ingenious solution. If you're talking to kids rather than adults, you might pick a different topic, but the technique would be the same for both of them.

ACT: Do you think a lot of children tend to be uneasy with science?

Herbert: My experience is that most children aren't really uncomfortable with science—at least, not the kind of science I do on my programs—because they are used to learning things. But it's different with adults. It's as though adults don't know how to learn any more; they assume that anything that's even the least bit "instructional" must be for children. We had a lot of adults react to the "How About" series by saying, enthusiastically, "I'd sure like my kids to see that," because they didn't want to admit they didn't already know something. I think it's when children reach their teens that they start to pick up the adult prejudice against learning. It's too bad.

ACT: Many people complain that television encourages its viewers to be passive learners. As a television teacher, do you find that a problem?

Herbert: I don't think so. In both the old "Mr. Wizard" and in "Mr. Wizard's World," I try to do experiments that the children can repeat at home. In fact, one of my standard sentences always begins, "Now, when you do this at home...." I'm always encouraging the viewers to experiment. Hundreds of adults have come up to me and said, "I remember when I used to watch your show when I was a kid; my mother would always get mad at me because I would go into the kitchen afterward and mess it all up." And I always ask them, "Did she *really* get mad?" And usually they admit, "No, she actually didn't care about the kitchen; she was glad I was doing the experiments."

ACT: When did you start being Mr. Wizard?

Herbert: It all started in 1951, the year I began the series. In those days I was doing radio in Chicago. Television had just come along, and I decided it was time to do something about television. It was a turning point in my life. I sat down to figure out what I could do best and then designed a show around it, and it turned out to be "Mr. Wizard." I took it around to various people and finally to a packaging company, run by Jules Power. He sold it to the Cereal Institute, and NBC put it on the air as a public affairs program. At the same time, I was the General Electric Progress Reporter; I did three-minute science progress reports on a CBS Sunday program hosted by Ronald Reagan. In fact, he and I ended up doing several commercials together, although most of the time he was in California, while I was based in New York.

As soon as "Mr. Wizard" started to catch on, we did the Mr. Wizard books. The first one was a description of the science experiments from the first six programs, so children could do them at home. The second book was also experiments, organized in a different way. Each of the thirteen chapters was about a different scientific field, like botany or medicine, to give a child a feel for the different areas of science. For example, in the chapter about zoology, we explained how to make a very elaborate ants' nest, with a damp sponge in it to help control the moisture level for the ants. We presented the whole question of the moisture content of the nest as a scientific problem, and, in solving it, the children got something of the feeling of what it's like to be a zoologist.

Then we started Mr. Wizard's Science Club; it had about 50,000 members throughout the country. The members got mimeographed sheets of experiments once a month. Eventually, we collected all those pages of experiments into a third Mr. Wizard book.

ACT: I know from talking to scientists and science writers that the old "Mr. Wizard" program really influenced their lives. Many of them feel it determined their careers.

Herbert: I've heard that statement over and over again, and it amazes me. I know television is a very powerful medium, but it seems strange and frightening—and pleasing too, of course—that a simple half hour of black and white television in the fifties and sixties could have had that kind of influence. I was completely unaware of it when we did the show.

I once got a letter from five Harvard University medical students. It seems these five guys were sitting around one night asking each other how they got interested in medicine, and every single one of them answered, "Mr. Wizard." So they wrote a joint letter to tell me. At Rockefeller University, where all the students are working toward research Ph.D.s in science and medicine, I have a good friend who handles admissions. One of his standard questions is, "How did you get interested in science?" And, in the sixties and seventies, about fifty percent of the applicants would answer, "Mr. Wizard." He got a big kick out of that because he'd always tell them, "Oh, Mr. Wizard. He's a friend of mine." And they'd say, amazed, "You know Mr. Wizard?"

ACT: What do you think is the future of science on TV?

Herbert: The trick is to make science interesting. And that isn't as easy as it sounds. A teacher's job is to persuade students to learn—the work has to take place in the minds of the learners. That's why I try so hard to intrigue the TV viewers.

All through my career, I've been trying to understand what it is that makes something both entertaining and educational. I'm always trying to combine the two, to show that they don't have to be mutually exclusive. But of course there's no single way to mix education and entertainment so that they appeal to everyone. Each time I make a show I learn a little more about what makes science interesting to the general public; every show gives me a different answer. That's one of the reasons I still enjoy it so much, after all these years.

BEYOND DOCTOR BUNSEN HONEYDEW

Philip Morrison and Phylis Morrison

T he frequent appearances of Muppet Labs spokesman Dr. Bunsen Honeydew and his long-enduring aide Beaker follow a pattern: the lab coat, the
glib promise of an unwanted boon, and in the end, the damaging side effects.
The source of this image of TV science is painfully clear: it is the science of
the TV commercial, treated with the rueful cynicism of the Henson show.
That it is the prevalent, even dominant, view of science on TV is certain. For
television is, after all, ad-driven. Yet science is too influential in life to leave
wholly to the ads and their satirists.

Television viewers, adults as well as children, already possess a real, in-
ternal science of their own, one that owes nothing to the advertiser. Most
people who have had schooling up to the high school level and beyond have
developed a scientific outlook that contains an overlay of acceptable modern
words concealing a naive and long-serviceable faith in simple observations
and categorizations. Of course they will tell you the earth moves, but they see
the sun do so. Some of them know of novelties such as hormones, computer
chips, and DNA, but they view the whole structure of science as a magical set
of black boxes, rather than a series of interrelated concepts. Verbal and visual
symbols they have learned—the atomic formula for water, for example, or
the colors of the spectrum. But conceptually, they know little except from direct experience. Their attitude toward science is not so different from that of
an Athenian citizen, except that the latter might have watched the sky and
understood the crops better than our city folk.

Schools and the media take much blame for this lack of understanding.
In a world of people far from the roots of science, these institutions have not
nurtured those roots but have instead emphasized the novel, the fruits of long
endeavor, and the need for expertise. The roots of science, like those of technology, extend deep into the past, before instrumentation, even before writing. Understanding the order of seasons and sky, the growth of living things,
the weather (some TV weather reports come closer to science than any other

*Philip Morrison, Ph.D., is Institute Professor and professor of physics at the Massa-
chusetts Institute of Technology.*
Phylis Morrison teaches science and art to teachers and children.

programs) is part of these roots. Even the geologists of the pioneer days, like Charles Darwin himself, used very few instruments. They ordered everyday perceptions to build a scheme. That would seem to be the essence of science, even today, though now most of our data come out of perceptions mediated by machines. And dealing with information won via instruments creates its own special problems.

Technology deserves to be considered in any discussion of science and the media, since science and technology lie so close to one another. Only the aim of technology differs: to perform some useful act, not to gain insight. Science and technology feed each other in unending mutuality, and today's technology demands understanding—in other words, science—at almost every step of its development. The confluence of the two fields that is a habit of the media is, therefore, understandable, even if somewhat confusing.

With its air of the traditional, craftsmanship is another relevant part of technology that lies rather farther from science than most of technology today. The knowledge of a craftsman, working to a pattern learned long ago, with a strong instinctual sense of just what to do—a skill held, as it were, in the bones—is not the same as scientific understanding, though it might lead to science in time. Because interest in crafts is already widespread, the crafts—from cooking to gardening to ceramics—deserve explicit links to science. They should be used to stimulate questions, the answers to which lead, eventually, to scientific understanding.

The most troubling attribute of science as presented in the media seems to be the alienation of its practice and practitioners from everyday people and life. Since science is held to be an intellectual activity, scientists are cast in a stereotypically intellectual image: the white coat, the absentmindedness, the myopia of the zealous researcher. In keeping with the intimidating stereotype, scientific instruments are left as a mystery, yet portrayed as indispensable.

The treatment of the space shots a decade ago is instructive. Nothing was made out to be simple; the astronauts were shown as masters of a vast array of switches and controls. One day a delay in the action meant a TV fill-in. By good luck, someone chose to fill time with an engineer who did nothing more or less striking than throw liquid air on the floor, where it made the fine smoky vapors seen at every space shot, recalling the times in winter when the cold air turns the exhaled breath white. The engineer explained that when the cryogenic liquid leaked cold vapor out of the rocket vents, the damp Cape air yielded these vapors. This simple explanation was absolutely new to the TV reporters who had watched those vapors hour after hour without attempting any understanding. The complexity of the space shots had meant to the reporters, and to their viewers and readers, that the science involved was inexplicably sophisticated. No effort had been made to link the experiences of the astronauts with familiar matters. Instead, both the NASA

Experiments performed by Dr. Bunsen Honeydew (r.) and his assistant, Beaker, parody TV commercials' approach to science. *Copyright © 1979 Henson Associates, Inc. Reprinted with permission.*

scientists and the press seemed to be trying to prove that science and high technology are intrinsically separate from everyday life.

Television makes science intimidating in other ways. For example, it frequently shows us the wonders of undersea life, reminding us of all that is amazing about the natural world. This is indeed valid. But we rarely encounter any TV programs that suggest that the squirrels and pigeons of the neighborhood can be watched and identified as individuals and that their behavior can be, in some part, understood. It is true that television, as theater, often requires the exotic, the surprising. But not always. Chemistry is in the kitchen, physics is on the ball field, animal behavior lies down there where the ants crawl, physiology beats in one's own pulse, archaeology is layered in the neighborhood's waste baskets, and electrons and magnetic fields interact in your own TV tube. A balance of the strange and the familiar needs repeatedly to be represented. It is just this unifying power of science that enables us to see everyday events in the exciting context of the most far-flung adventures, and to see scientific adventures in the homely context of day-to-day phenomena.

The most important lesson that science programming can teach children—and indeed most adults—is that authority alone does not make knowledge. The chance to learn from the natural and the ordinary is lost if a long chain of credentials is invariably placed between the phenomenon and the learner. Perhaps this is the touchstone of good media science: without denying the excitement of the expert exploring the unusual, there must be ample evidence that science can be pursued in more familiar surroundings, using simple observation and common sense.

Another way that TV producers make science mysterious is with the use of too many abstract terms and concepts. What is science today without energy, without atoms, without computers? So a lot of words are dedicated in the name of science to discussing these things, yet the words are never defined and the phenomena themselves never explained. Much that is poorly understood and poorly expressed passes for science if it is disguised with big words. Atoms and energy are difficult concepts; there is a lot to learn before they become more than abstractions. The need of people, birds, trees, molds, and automobiles for some essential nutrient is an idea that predates the words "atom" and "energy." The first sensible question to ask when one is concerned with energy—whether one is talking about pendulums, birds, or automobiles—is: What do they eat? The answers to questions like this are easy to visualize, familiar, and rather fun. Have they ever been discussed this way in the media?

There are two parts to any work in science: method (or process) and subject matter. In our view, the two must be interwoven. The fusion is alive; but either one by itself faces the danger of being reduced to a lifeless list of facts. To focus on "the scientific method" alone, as if it were a recipe, denies the years of thought and experiment and the unique combination of chance, sudden enlightenment, and blunder that lead to the formation of a good hypothesis in the first place. Did Kepler already have elliptical orbits in mind when he began to observe the movements of the planets? Or Darwin start out to test natural selection?

To concentrate on subject matter alone is also limiting. For example, everyone who demonstrates how a prism breaks light into bands of color begins by darkening the room, leaving only a single beam of light to pass through the prism. Yet the same demonstration could teach something about scientific methods as well as about its subject matter—the light spectrum—if it were first attempted in a brilliantly lit room. The prism's effect on white light would be difficult, if not impossible, to observe in a well-lit room, and the demonstration would fail. The demonstration's failure would explain far better than words the problems that interfering factors or "noise"—in this case, extraneous light—can create in an experiment. A key methodological step in science, the isolation of a single factor, is thus made meaningful by example rather than narration.

Television programming that illustrates the methodology of science as well as its subject matter is important for another reason: it reveals the place of error in scientific inquiry. To be in error is not the worst thing, if the path that leads to identifying the error increases understanding. Scientists are always having to face up to error; even the best of them will get something wrong sooner or later. Having doubts can be more important than acknowledging errors. That we don't know, or that we can't tell, is sometimes the very best conclusion. That admission says more of the method of science—of its tolerance for doubt and indecision, of its need for testing, of its incompleteness—than much discussion about hypotheses and well-polished tests.

What we would hope to see when we turn on our TV consists in large part of things already there: the National Geographic's distant journeys, the close-up studies of exotic animals, the demonstrations of the computer industry's latest breakthroughs, the lift-off of a rocket. Such wonders are worthy of display; they are part and parcel of science in action. What would make them far more valuable is a direct connection to our experience. The connection could be verbal, done by deliberate narration, or better, it could be done indirectly, alternating the reporting of wonders with examples of everyday experience so as to convey the unity of science. One prerequisite for this kind of media science is time, even if only enough time for instant replays, slow motion, fast forward, or whatever production trick is needed to convert something grand into something understandable. Sports broadcasters have learned that it takes time and repetition to make the great plays and close calls accessible to the audience. The programs that explain science should use the same creativity in their presentations.

Many of the learning experiences in science can be connected to our own lives, giving us the power to test them, question them, and add them to what we already know. The concepts and products of science may be as exotic as the ends of the universe, but the sense of belief and satisfaction that comes from understanding them demands a link with the eye and the hand. It is always there in science, that link, we know. The art of popular science is to forge the chain of inference simply—no easy task. Perhaps we would prefer that, for young viewers especially, the topics of science programming be chosen and handled with that long chain of connections in mind. To explain about the atom, for example, we must first explore its history through chemistry. To explain energy, we must talk about the familiar concepts of consumption and nutrition. How exactly to convey these connections using all of the tricks and arts of television production is the exciting challenge facing the producers of television science of the future. Good luck to them. They have a world to win.

BREAD, LOVE, AND GAPESEED*: REFLECTIONS OF A FORMER CHILD

Josephine Gladstone

Though city-raised, I had country instincts. At the age of eight, growing up in the Borough of Hammersmith, London, I was allowed to visit the local natural history museum alone every Saturday morning. There, along with a small group of other city kids whom I got to know slightly, I learned to draw stuffed birds, trapped many years earlier and preserved for posterity by the taxidermist's art. The variation in these little birds' coloring, the differences in plumage between the males and the females in each species, the shape of their claws and beaks in relation to their diets, and their adaptations to the strange thickets and shores that they inhabited all called forth the full weight of my enthusiasm. I do not think I had heard the name of Charles Darwin at that time.

The intensity of my interest did not convey itself in the clumsy drawings I made each week on the museum papers we were handed in our informal bird study group. But no one minded that. The fact was that, for me, being greeted by a robust teenage guide in the Gothic museum hall each Saturday was the moment I longed for all week. We were handed our inky wooden clipboards, our museum pencils, and a little pack of chewed Crayolas, and we were off, like greyhounds coursing the electric hare. The rest of the morning was bliss. So was the next Saturday, and the next, and the next.

One summer not too long after the bird-sketching Saturdays, I started keeping a nature diary. Although my colors were more refined by then than the museum Crayolas, the diary was a frustration to me. It seemed to move

Josephine Gladstone is a producer in the National Film Division of WGBH Educational Foundation in Boston. She contributed to the production of the BBC's "Horizon" and "The Ascent of Man" series and WGBH's "Tales of a Medical Life" and "A Festival of Hands." She is currently developing a documentary film series with Mike Latham and Dr. June Goodfield called "From the Face of the Earth."

*gapeseed: anything to feed the eye or idly gape after, such as rope dancers, monsters, and mountebanks. Definition from *A New Canting Dictionary*[1], 1725.

Learning by discovering is what science is all about: that's one of the messages of the instructional series "Discovering," made for classroom use. *Photo courtesy of Agency for Instructional Television.*

forward so slowly. Was it that I could perceive very little of note in nature that summer? In any case, I did manage to jot down one or two things. One time I saw a dolphin leap clear out of the blue waters of Bantry Bay; another time I realized that those were wild hops crawling all over the shed in the back yard.

I have stayed keen on the life sciences ever since. But it was not my school studies, my museum visits, or even my nature diary that confirmed my commitment. It was television. Soon after I started keeping my diary, Queen Elizabeth II was crowned. The ceremony was very long, but we watched it all on a rented black-and-white TV that sat in the middle of our drawing room floor. Once in the habit, my family started to use the TV with some frequency. Then it happened. Along with child viewers all over the country, I began to watch the low-budget natural history series presented by James Fisher once a week. The emphasis of the program was bird-watching. It was only barely television; a good deal of it could have been done on the radio, as I well knew even at the time. Dr. Fisher talked a good deal "to camera," but he did have two constant guests, colleagues of his in the bird-watching line of business. One could imitate bird calls so mellifluously that had he been on the radio, you would have sworn he was actually a bird. The other was a fast-moving bird artist. He drew, even with clumsy charcoal, the private life of the gannet with such precision and panache that he quite took your breath away.

Imagine my surprise a few weeks later when Dr. Fisher (a scientist of the Bronowski school who deeply believed that the public should care about the scientific enterprise in all its manifestations) asked the audience to send in any nature notes we might have been keeping in recent months. I did not even stop to think. I put my nature diary in an envelope and mailed it with that same glow of assurance that I had felt every Saturday as I hurried to the museum. Something good was going on. Something better might be just around the corner.

I was lucky. Soon afterward, there came hurtling back through the mail-slot in my front hall my nature diary, with a bulky enclosure. James Fisher, my TV hero, had sent me his two-volume bird-watching book. It was so grown-up and so extremely boring that it was put away until I grew older. But that is not the point. He had signed it himself and had greeted me in the inscription as a fellow nature lover. I was overwhelmed: somebody who really knew what he was talking about cared! That massive, untidy field of human investigation known as biology would remain forever in my sight, would have my constant support. The recruit for science was won—and won by that little black-and-white television set in the middle of the drawing room floor.

Since those days, the science genie has been coaxed out of the broadcasting bottle by a talented handful of visionary producers, and the adult market has been confirmed forever on both sides of the Atlantic. Minor funding setbacks will not alter the picture. Science programming for children, however, along with the rest of children's programming, is in a more delicate state. Its potential is obvious nevertheless. For proof, one need only look at the output of England's BBC-TV, one broadcasting system that has both longevity and a future.

BBC-I broadcasts about 820 hours a year exclusively for children. This output is seen by about ten million young people. The audience constitutes seventeen percent of the viewing public, a force to be reckoned with if only on a numerical basis. Original programming produced by over forty full-time children's producers makes up half of BBC-I's annual children's output. The average production budget is not enviable: approximately $32,000 an hour. However, these budgets and the children's programs they are designed to pay for are inviolable, as children's programming on BBC has been since 1922 when the network was set up.

Typical of the children's programs carried by the network is "Blue Peter," a series that shares the interests of the British Royal Family: sailing, large pets, and good form. Lately, however, some valuable diversification has begun, identified by the head of children's programs in the following terms:

> We produce our own drama, current affairs, news, situation comedy, sports, light entertainment, art, music, and [wait for it!] natural history.[2]

(Has the head of BBC children's programs never heard of science broadcasting? Of course he has. It is just that "natural history" makes science sound less earnest.) Some of this newer BBC-I programming, then, has room for science. For example, a delightful do-it-yourself series that is not as self-defeating as its title would suggest ("Why Don't You Turn Off Your TV Set and Do Something Less Boring Instead?") marks a trend toward viewer involvement that the U.S. might do well to emulate. Science and medical items, specially chosen and developed by a team of researchers, also make their way onto the very popular "John Craven's News Round," a news service especially devoted to children's interests.

In keeping with the general trend toward a more thorough sense of reality observed by educators among students, some of the young people's science broadcasting that is doing well in the U.K. consists of plain, if lively, didacticism. Examples are a children's series about astronomy, "Heavens Above," and a trilogy about computers featuring Monty Python's John Cleese, who explains technology with a good deal of help from a cartoon character called "The Monk."

Despite these noteworthy efforts to bring science and children together through television, however, the United Kingdom shares with the United

States a failure to adequately teach science to young people. A recent survey of primary schools finds that "there is an absence of emphasis in teaching on the more science-oriented skills" and concludes that "teachers may not be providing for scientific experience. . . . It is not, then, surprising that the essential nature of primary science as a process of enquiry has not been carried forward to any degree in the work of the pupils."[3]

Of course, as Alistair Cooke has pointed out, this kind of criticism reflects a general indictment of looser and more permissive educational techniques that has been going on for centuries, in response to educators as profound as Jean-Jacques Rousseau and John Dewey. Cooke, who believes that some such criticism is merited, identifies the problem with characteristic candor:

> John Dewey's *The School and Society* manifesto of 1899 invoked the banishment of slavery from education and promised enlightenment, spontaneity, the identification of the child with his studies in a new and passionate way. . . . The study of historical periods was supplanted by trips into Fenimore Cooper country to bring home to the budding New Yorker the very touch and smell of the life of Algonquin Indians. I have known children who left school with a vivid knowledge of the way the earliest inhabitants of Manhattan lived and ordered society, even if they had never heard of the Bill of Rights, a hanging participle, or the Thirty Years War.[4]

Or, he might have added if he had been more alert to the need for science education, an electron. For, whether in school or via television, spectatorism is not enough by itself. It must be supplemented by involvement between individuals—by that extra boost to the self-confidence that a caring teacher, sibling, or friend can give a child who is caught up in the learning process. It is not enough to lean on the notion—a form of New Primitivism—that deep instinct will guide young people to scientific understanding. Crucial to kindling that instinct is the guidance of genially disposed practitioners with experience of science greater than the young viewer. It must, in part, be through such hands-on guidance that young people will find their way to a deeper appreciation of science, whether it be through nature diaries, clumsy drawings of birds, science television programs, or anything else that captures their enthusiasm.

The words of educator and philosopher Jean-Jacques Rousseau remind us of how much we stand to gain if we take our responsibilities to our children seriously. After Rousseau had spelled out his long Enlightenment dream to educate the orphaned Émile, child of his brain though not of his body, he rested a while and withdrew from his self-appointed task, and this is what he said:

> Whatever he may become in the future, whatever fortune grants or takes from him, what no one will ever be able to deprive him of is what I gave him. I cannot have wasted my time, for I have made him into a man. I hope he will fulfill his duty on earth. As for me, I have done mine.[5]

Scientists, educators, television program makers, politicians, and former children, have we done ours? What will little Émile and his female counterpart Sophie think of us when they grow up if we fail them now? What can we do that we are not doing at present to enhance the understanding of the potential and hazards of science and technology in our time? What can television do to help restore the confidence children should have in their own aptitudes for science and its forms of investigation, discovery, and entrancement?

Television, which helped to create our spectator mentality, can also help us to surpass it. We cannot leave the responsibility for teaching our children exclusively with the educational institutions of the past, for the supplies of Crayolas in the museums and schools of our cities are running low. Why not mobilize all the media, from crayons and canned bird song to videotape and film, for the education and delight of our twentieth-century Sophies and Émiles, in an age when science is king?

NOTES

1. *A New Canting Dictionary, comprehending all the terms, ancient and modern, used in the several tribes of gypsies, beggars, shoplifters, highwaymen, footpads, and all other clans of cheats and villains* (London: 1725).

2. Patrick Campbell, "Children's Programming: Will the British Programmers Play at Innovation?" *TV World* (August 1982): 11–18.

3. Department of Education and Science, *Primary Education in England: A Survey by Her Majesty's Inspectors of Schools* (London: Her Majesty's Stationary Office, 1978).

4. Alistair Cooke, "Where the Difference Begins," *The Permissive Society: The Guardian Enquiry* (London: Penguin Books, 1969) 58–61.

5. Jean-Jacques Rousseau, *Émile ou L'Education*, Bernard Gerland and Danielle Gerland, eds. (Montrouge, France: Bordas, 1973).

A KIDSEYE VIEW OF THE PERFECT SCIENCE TV SHOW

Fred Jerome

Imagine, if you can, a television network executive who decides that our society would benefit from a good children's TV show about science. Imagine that this executive has become so concerned about the low level of scientific literacy in this country and the dreadful state of science education in our classrooms that he is willing to disregard the low "market value" of a twelve-year-old audience and spend the money on a quality program for the sake of the public good. Imagine that he cares enough about the success of this new venture to ask a number of children to write to him about what they'd like to see in such a program.

If your imagination can stretch far enough to conceive all of that, you should have no trouble imagining this reply from one seventh-grader.

Dear TV Network Executive:

You asked what I'd like to see in a TV show about science. First of all, it should be fun. If it's boring, I'd rather watch cartoons, even though cartoons get boring too, sometimes. Still, a good science program should have cartoons. I once saw a cartoon movie in school about white blood cells, and the movie made them look like Pac-Man swallowing up the germs, and then there were these vaccine things that looked like germs but weren't as strong. That would be good for a kids' science TV show.

You should get someone like Bill Cosby to be the host. He's got five kids and has made a lot of funny records for kids. He knows how to explain things without lecturing so that you understand them and can still laugh at the same time. I know he's not a scientist, but he could have guests who are

Fred Jerome is the director of the Media Resource Service, a program of the Scientists' Institute for Public Information. He is also an adjunct professor of journalism at New York University and the School of Visual Arts and has published numerous articles on science and the media. His main qualifications for writing this essay, however, are Rebecca, 17, Mark, 15, and Daniel, 13, all of whom contributed to its preparation.

"Universe and I" is an instructional series designed to stimulate junior high school students' enthusiasm about science. In this program, Leonard Nimoy plays a Victorian detective who solves scientific mysteries. The series is distributed by Agency for Instructional Television. *Photo courtesy of the Kentucky Educational Television Photo Department, © KET.*

scientists and people like Isaac Asimov who have written good science books for children.

Then you should have two or three kids on the show with Bill Cosby. They should be about twelve years old, boys and girls. When there are experiments on the show, it would be good to have the kids do them so that we would feel we could do them, too. Kids can help explain things to other kids in a way that adults just can't, and they ask the kinds of questions that we want to ask. And Bill Cosby is very funny when he's with kids. Whatever you do, don't have some grown-up get up there and just tell us things. We get that all day in school. Usually, I'm so busy writing down what the teacher is telling us—we're supposed to take notes in school—that I don't have time to think about the questions I want to ask. (My uncle says the teacher plans it that way.)

The most important thing you should do is get kids who are watching at home to be part of the program. There are lots of ways you could do this. For example:

- *Questions.* We should be able to write in questions about science. Bill Cosby could read the questions and give a funny answer, first, if he wanted to, and then a scientist could show (not just tell) the answer. If too many questions come in to be answered on TV, someone from the program could write back with the answers. Also, there should be some time on each show when we could call in—live!—with questions. In school, it seems like the teachers always ask the questions and we have to give the answers on tests.

- *Debates.* People think we aren't interested in things like nuclear power or acid rain or whether you should eat hot dogs. But that's not true. You could have an argument between two sides of questions like that, with scientists on each side trying to convince us. Only please don't have them just talking *at* us. They should use pictures and movies to explain their cases. At the end, you could use a telephone-voting system to see what the audience thinks. That would be exciting—only don't charge fifty cents for each call or my parents won't let me vote.

- *Mystery.* Have you ever read the books about Encyclopedia Brown? Well, he's this brainy kid who comes in and solves all kinds of mysteries in his neighborhood by seeing clues that are hard to see and putting them all together. Before explaining the solution, the books ask you to guess the answer. (Then you turn to another page to find out.) It makes you think. And it's exciting and fun. Each story is only a few pages long. You could do the same thing with science. Plan mysteries where the kid who is the detective would use scientific clues to figure out the

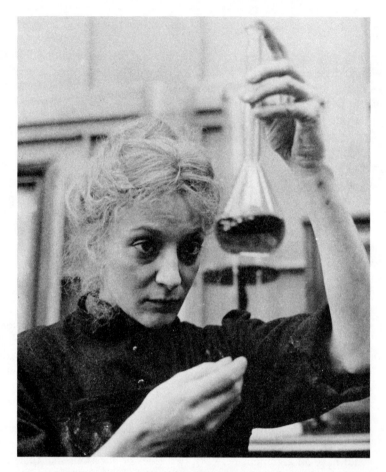

"Marie Curie," a series produced by BBC/Time-Life and aired on PBS, dramatized the life of the discoverer of radium. Jane Lapotaire plays the title role of the famous scientist. *Copyright © BBC.*

answers. That could include basic science stuff you learn at school, like hot air rising or water expanding when it turns to ice, and also laboratory experiments, like Quincy does on TV. Before the crime or mystery was solved, the kids in the audience could be asked what they think. You could have a call-in contest with a prize for the first right answer, and the prize should be that the winner gets to be on the program.

- *Special Guests.* You should have people like Quincy on as special guests. It would be great to find out how he studied to get ready for a program. You could have a rock star showing how music is made, or an astronaut, or an athlete like Reggie Jackson or Larry Bird showing how they throw baseballs or shoot baskets. Then someone could explain (with pictures and cartoons) the science behind what makes a curveball curve. Or how about a special guest like R2D2 from *Star Wars*, or even better, E.T.? They could talk about outer space. And you could take four or five calls each time from kids at home who want to ask the guest a question.

You wouldn't have to have all these things on every program, but they should come on regularly, say, every other week or something like that.

I guess by now you can tell that I'm big on the idea of calling in. It would be something new for a kids' show, and it would be an example of how modern science works. Also, it would really make us feel like we're a part of the program. But there are also other things you could have to make the show exciting. Here are some suggestions:

- *How do things work?* When I ask my parents how the picture gets on the TV set or how the voice comes over the telephone, they usually say, "Ask your science teacher." If I get a chance to ask my science teacher, he usually says, "It's too complicated to explain right now, we'll get to it later." You could do one thing each week—television, telephone, records, cars, the space shuttle, and even video games like Pac-Man (what goes on inside the computer?)—and explain how it works with movies and cartoons. You could have the kids on the show do simple experiments as part of the explanation. They should be experiments we could do at home, just like those cooking lessons on TV.

- *How do we work?* How do we see things? Why do we get tired? Why do we get colds? How does the brain work? What do drugs do to you? I'd love to see Stevie Wonder and learn how he hears and how we hear. (Can blind people really hear better?) This part of the show could also explain things about nutrition and the food we eat. My uncle told me pizza is really the most nutritious breakfast you could have. Is that true? (I hope so).

- *How do scientists discover things?* In my science book, they always show pictures of famous scientists (usually men with beards) who discovered things like bacteria or electricity or the way an atom is built. We're supposed to memorize their names and the dates, and then we have to get them right on a test. Boring! It would be interesting to see how these people really discovered things. You could have a play about the life of one of these famous scientists. It could show the problems he (or she) had with his family and friends and with people who laughed at him or didn't like what he was doing, and the problems he had trying experiments that didn't work. A bunch of plays like this would be neat. They should be exciting and not too long. My teacher told us about a book called *Microbe Hunters* that has some stories like this. Maybe you could use that.

- **What scientists don't know.** In school, you always get the feeling that the answer to everything is in the science book. Or in the scientists' heads. But my uncle says that there are a lot of things that scientists don't know yet. Like how a baby grows from one single cell or how we remember things or what's out there beyond the universe or how the world began. You could have a short part in some of the programs about these questions. You could show what scientists don't know yet, or what they think the answers might be and what they're doing to try to find out. That would give us something to think about—and it wouldn't make us feel like we're the only ones who don't know things. Besides, maybe somebody in the audience might come up with an answer the scientists haven't thought of. Or maybe some of us will decide to *be* scientists when we grow up so we can do experiments and find out answers.

- **UFOs and stuff.** Lots of my friends talk about UFOs and whether or not they're real and come from other planets. And also about things like the Bermuda Triangle. Does it really swallow up boats and planes? And ESP, and people who say they can bend spoons with their brainwaves, and people who say they've come back from the dead, and other stuff like that. I wondered about those things, too, and then we got this book called *Flim Flam* by James Randi. He used to be a magician, but now he goes around explaining how all these so-called supernatural things are really fakes. He even offered to pay $10,000 to anyone who could do a supernatural feat in front of him that he couldn't explain. I think it would be fun to have him come on a show, say, once a month, to explain some of these things. You could show a rerun of a part of "Real People" or "That's Incredible!" where they have some guy who says he's been dead. Then James Randi could explain it. I know my friends would watch this.

- **New inventions.** Each week you could show some new invention or discovery scientists have come up with. This part shouldn't be too long, but it would be interesting and help us keep up with what's going on.

Some of these ideas were on "3-2-1 Contact," which was a pretty good show. Too bad more kids didn't watch it. There's another thing—no matter what you do, it's going to be hard to get kids or even grown-ups to watch a science show. When kids hear the word "science" a lot of us get turned off. We think it's going to be more dull school science that doesn't seem to have anything to do with our lives.

So even if the show is good and exciting, it will need a lot of commercials on TV to let people know about it, especially in the beginning. For instance, Bill Cosby could come on and ask the audience something like, "How do you know the earth isn't flat?" Or, "Did you ever dream of flying without a plane? Is it possible?" And then he could say, "To find out, tune in. . . ."

Oh yes, 7:30 at night would be a good time. Then grown-ups could watch it, too, if they wanted. The only problem is that teachers might assign it as homework. Then it wouldn't be as much fun!

I'm sure you could get a lot more suggestions from other kids. I hope this letter wasn't too long. But you did ask me for my ideas. That's something nobody has ever done before.

SCIENCE IN THE
SCHOOLS

*Only one third of the country's 17,000 school districts re-
quire more than one year of mathematics and science for high
school graduation.*

National Science Foundation
Today's Problems: Tomorrow's Crises
October 1982

Only the most fanatic advocate of television would ever suggest that TV programs about science can substitute for classroom instruction. As a number of the authors in this volume point out, no long-distance learning experience can replace the personal relationship between teacher and student. But if good teaching can make a major difference in children's attitudes toward science, so, unfortunately, can bad teaching.

In this chapter, three educators examine the ways that science is taught in elementary and secondary school. Juliana Texley, a high school science teacher and editor of *The Science Teacher*, describes how creative teachers over the past thirty years have used television to help them make science come alive. Jeffry Mallow, associate professor of physics at Loyola University and developer of the country's first science anxiety clinic, shows how poor instruction can be one of the causes of aversion to science. Finally, Paul Hurd, professor emeritus of education at Stanford and a specialist in science education who has been a consultant to the National Science Foundation, writes a jeremiad which proves that the problem of science in our schools is not going to go away; in fact, it appears to be getting worse.

USING TV IN THE SCIENCE CLASS

Juliana Texley

The teaching of science is not all science. Despite volumes of educational research, there exists no single theory or method that most science teachers find effective for most students. Trends in instruction periodically change; specific methods gain in popularity while others fall into disuse. In the real world of the classroom, the teacher juggles the demands of students, administrators, home, and community while coping with a rapidly growing knowledge base. In the final analysis, the process of teaching is at least as much art as science. The dynamic relationship between teacher and student defies quantification.

This relationship is both fragile and tenuous. Classroom hours represent only a fraction of a child's day. Even within the schoolroom walls, the distractions of administrative procedures steal precious time from the instructional process. The average elementary school child spends from twenty to thirty minutes a day studying science;[1] a secondary-school science period may be fifty-five minutes long. Within that time, the instructor takes attendance, writes passes, reads announcements, disciplines students, administers fund raisers, provides make-up materials—and teaches the content and processes of science.

The "artistic" teacher instinctively capitalizes on the knowledge and experience students bring with them to school as the building blocks of learning. But the experiences of today's students are as different from those of their predecessors as today's science is from the science of the pre-World War II era. Students today have the mental baggage of thousands of hours of vicarious exploration with that other teacher, television. They are more sophisticated, harder to amaze or shock, and more easily bored with material less current than last night's newscast. Their ties to books are less secure than those of previous generations of students. Perhaps most importantly, constant exposure to major events and fantastic happenings on TV often denies today's young people that sense of wonder at the small things of the world

Juliana Texley, *Ph.D.*, *is a high school science teacher and editor of* The Science Teacher, *the secondary school journal of the National Science Teachers Association.*

around us—the opening of a flower or the appearance of the dew—that motivated previous generations to study science.

Does this mean that television is the enemy? Not necessarily. As teachers reach for methods through which they can motivate today's science students, they often find that television can be a powerful ally. There have been thirty years of television kids, and thirty years of educational research telling teachers how to motivate them. At least three styles of teaching have gained and lost favor during these three decades, and each found its complement in a style of television!

In the 1950s, the "traditional" teacher relied on extrinsic rewards (grades, approval, evaluations) as motivators. The "ideal classroom" scenario involved:

- dramatic demonstrations;

- structured textbooks;

- emphasis on the "facts" science has revealed;

- evaluations based on knowledge and comprehension.

The underlying psychology was behavioral; the premier researcher B.F. Skinner. The science of the 1950s provided answers to all man's questions. The science teacher, in popular view, was the person who provided answers to students.

During these years, a video teacher epitomized the best in science instruction. Don Herbert, as Mr. Wizard, demonstrated the amazing facts of science to on-screen observers from 1951 to 1965. Some of his most faithful viewers were teachers in search of new and better demonstrations. A volcano that spewed sparks and ash, a gallon can that collapsed on cue, an eyedropper that rose and fell at the teacher's command: each splashy demonstration was sure to start a series of questions from students. Why? How? Will it happen again? In the "expository mode" of instruction favored in the 1950s, the teacher followed each demonstration with a selection from the text or a lecture. No good teacher would do a demonstration he or she was not prepared to explain.

Television science, playing the role of "The Answer Man," was certainly a powerful ally in the science classrooms of the 1950s. But by 1962, the preferred mode of science education had changed. Answers had gone out of style. "Inquiry" was in.

In 1958, Jean Piaget, the Swiss psychologist, told teachers that the motivation for scientific discovery was intrinsic in puzzling experiences. Teachers should not provide answers or rely on rewards; rather, they should facilitate contact with unanswered questions in the environment. This was the teach-

Still going strong today in syndication, "Star Trek" created a cult of dedicated viewers in the 1960s, and helped some teachers turn science fiction into science learning. Here, Captain Kirk (William Shatner), Mr. Spock (Leonard Nimoy), and Dr. McCoy (DeForest Kelley) stand ready to be "beamed down" to yet another strange planet. *Photo courtesy of Paramount Pictures. Copyright © 1966 Paramount Pictures Corp. All rights reserved.*

ing mode dubbed "inquiry," the style favored by the government-backed curriculum innovators of the 1960s.

During the sixties, science class was less likely to begin with an explosion from a make-believe volcano than with the burning of a single candle. "How many characteristics (properties) can you see?" the teacher/facilitator might have asked. "What color is the flame?" "How does it flicker?" The end product of the lesson was not knowledge of beeswax oxidation; rather, it was the students' skills at observation that were being honed.

Observation was the first in a lengthy list of science processes recommended to curriculum designers by the prestigious American Association for the Advancement of Science.[2] That the process was the end rather than the means of the new programs was evident when one considers a common fi-

"The Undersea World of Jacques Cousteau" is a prime-time series that many teachers have used in their classrooms. This scene is from "The Smile of the Walrus." *Photo courtesy of Metromedia Producers Corporation.*

nale to the candle burning experiment. Often, when the students finished their list of observations, they found that their senses had been fooled. What was burning was not a candle at all, it was a peanut implanted in a cylinder of potato! Whether the experience in question was the reproduction rate of yeast, the behavior of mealworms, or the shadows cast by a sundial, the common denominators of inquiry-based lessons were unstructured investigations and unanswered questions.

Television programming that would supplement the inquiry-based curricula was harder to find. At first glance, it seemed inconceivable that programming which challenged the viewer to think, but then denied explanation, would ever become common on commercial networks. Would anyone pay to be disequilibrated, a term Piaget used to describe the mental discomfort of a puzzling experience?

While educational television hesitated, one segment of television in the 1960s was demonstrating a willingness to end on the interrogative "What if?". That was, and still is, science fiction. While most educational television programs provided answers, television science fiction asked questions, and as it did, it complemented the inquiry role of science teaching.

Science fiction shows challenged existing mind-sets, provoked unanswered questions, and left the viewer wondering. The TV phoenix "Star Trek" was a prime example. Science for Trekkies? Why not? The Gene Roddenberry production explored population control, racial stereotypes, nuclear and biological warfare, and the relative worth of cognitive versus affective values, leaving issues for the viewer to answer:

- If life can be based on carbon, might it also be based on silicon, an element in the same group on the periodic table?

- Could a living cell exist that was light years in diameter? Could the surface area of the membrane support the cytoplasmic volume? If it did, might it eat planets as food through pinocytosis?

- If the planetary environments were similar, might very different forms of life develop along similar lines through convergent evolution?

If, in the spirit of inquiry, the viewer was disequilibrated, so much the better. The confident teacher welcomed science fiction and inquiry-based education into the classroom at the same time.

But many teachers were not so confident. The ultimate failure of the total inquiry approach has been blamed on poorly prepared teachers, budget cuts, "back to basics" movements, and declining reading levels among students.[3] Some have even blamed the demise of the 1960s curricula on television. No matter what the reason, the end result was a movement in science education back to center.

Today's teacher has the best techniques of both the expository curricula and the inquiry-based programs from which to choose. The new watchword to guide the motivation of today's science students, however, is relevance. The impact of technology upon society is receiving increased attention in the literature,[4] and teachers are often told, "Use the techniques that work best for you, but make them relevant!"

Just as educational methods have returned to some sort of middle road, a new sort of "hybrid" television programming has appeared and made its impact on the classroom. Shows which offer a blend of science fact and science fiction have captured the enthusiasm of young viewers. A typical classroom dialogue:

Mrs. Smith, did you see the mouse that breathed under liquid on "That's Incredible!"?

Yes, I did; tell the class about it and then we can all discuss how it might be possible.

Pity the poor teacher who spent the previous evening doing lesson plans! The new "amazing science" programs effectively blend the latest in technological advances with a bit of speculation and a healthy dose of puzzlement. They provide an up-to-the-minute counterpoint for today's science instruction. If the production of such shows is done with concern for accuracy, they can become valuable classroom partners. What can't be explained (by the science teacher or the scientist) is the subject for speculation and investigation. This is the stuff of which future careers are made.

But what of the perils of television for the young viewer? At various times since its inception, television has been accused of stifling the urge for exploration and research in young people, making them unduly passive.[5] Despite extensive research, hard evidence for this effect has failed to appear. But what has become evident to teachers is that TV programming and commercials contain a significant amount of inaccurate science and pseudoscience, often so intricately interwoven with fact as to be almost imperceptible to all but the most critical viewers:

> It's the acid in coffee that makes it bitter. (Any freshman chemist knows that acids are identified by a sour taste, and bases by bitterness.)

> Brand X mouthwash kills cold and strep throat germs. (But colds are caused by viruses; strep is a bacterium.)

In a TV world where viper jets roar in the blackness of outer space, it is often hard to convince young people that in a vacuum "no one can hear you scream." When young people watch TV characters cavort with dinosaurs, it becomes doubly hard to convey the relative proportions of the geologic time scale.[6] Despite the concerted efforts of various governmental and private groups, scientific misinformation in commercials and programs is bound to remain; there will be twenty-first-century wonder cures and endless reruns of "The Flintstones" for years to come. But teachers seem to have reached at least one consensus about television: It's here to stay so we might as well use it.

Supervised exposure to television—even television at its worst—provides a good opportunity for developing critical skills needed for both scientific research and intelligent television viewing. Programs of instruction in science have been built around advertising claims and product labels.[7] It seems clear that the emphasis on "real world science" in today's classroom is complemented by instruction in critical viewing skills. When what the child sees on TV is brought into the classroom to be analyzed, researched, or challenged, the goals of relevant curricula are achieved. Advertisers and programmers can assist by encouraging communication, being open about procedures and verification of claims, and providing documentation to would-be young skeptics. The lessons learned may produce lifelong skills.

Sometimes, the results of such a study go beyond a teacher's expectations. When one New York high school teacher asked his class (sophomore chemistry) to compare the effectiveness of various antacids, the students found that the "new, improved" brand wasn't any better than the unchanged, older version. They wrote the manufacturer to ask why. The firm responded, "You have not used the correct Food and Drug Administration procedure; amateurs should not attempt professional experimentation." Undaunted, the class (and a very patient instructor) proceeded to repeat their tests, carefully following FDA standards. Lo and behold, "new and improved" still fared no better. (Never underestimate the persistence of adolescents.) They went back to the manufacturer with the results. "How remarkable!" the firm replied. "Your results duplicate ours exactly." No word yet on the status of that advertising campaign. But thirty secondary school students will see television commercials in a different light for the rest of their lives.[8]

Today's science is expanding at a rate that often seems comprehensible only to computers. As the world beyond the text in hand accelerates in complexity, the few moments shared by teacher and student become increasingly inadequate. Tomorrow's teacher will need many media to expand the power of the learning process: microcomputers, laboratory tools, real world explorations, simulations—and television. To teachers still puzzled by conflicting data on methodology and the media, television provides a motivation in itself. For there is no denying that the tube demands a degree of attention from kids that few teachers can command.

Thus, television should not be seen as an interloper in the classroom. It can be both ally and subject of study. The artistic interweaving of television experience and classroom lesson has the potential to enrich the fabric of education as it multiplies the time spent on the learning process manyfold.

NOTES

1. Office of Scientific and Engineering Personnel and Education, *Science and Engineering Education: Data and Information* (Washington, D.C.: National Science Foundation, 1982).

2. American Association for the Advancement of Science, "Science: A Process Approach." Photocopied, 1970.

3. James Shymansky, William Kyle, Jr., and Jennifer Alport, "Alphabet Soup Science," *The Science Teacher* 49 (November 1982): 49–53.

4. Robert Yager, Avi Hoffstein, and Vincent Lunetta, "Science Education Attuned to Social Issues: Challenge for the 1980s," *The Science Teacher* 48 (December 1981): 12–13.

5. George Comstock *et al., Television and Human Behavior* (New York: Columbia University Press, 1978): 388.

6. John Renner, Margaret Brumby, and Debbie L. Shepherd, "Why Are There No Dinosaurs in Oklahoma?" *The Science Teacher* 48 (December 1981): 22–24.

7. Raj A. Rajan, "Product Labels—Ingredients for Chemistry Study," *The Science Teacher* 48 (December 1981): 28–30; Salvatore Tocci, "Over-the-Counter Chemistry," *The Science Teacher* 49 (November 1982): 45–48.

8. Salvatore Tocci, "Over-the-Counter Chemistry," *The Science Teacher* 49 (November 1982): 45–48.

SCIENCE ANXIETY

Jeffry V. Mallow

It is a truism that young children are by nature scientists: they possess boundless curiosity, they delight in discovery, and a large part of their intellectual development consists of manipulating objects in order to gain understanding of their local environment. Yet as children grow older and begin to study science in school, many if not most of them acquire a marked aversion to the subject. In fact, this aversion is frequently accompanied by so-called "science anxiety,"[1] a fear of not comprehending science that becomes a self-fulfilling prophecy. Students become so afraid of their inability to grasp the content of one or more of the sciences that they are unable to concentrate and consequently do poorly. This fear is so widespread that primary and secondary schools have lowered the science content in their curricula to the point where students can graduate from high school with only one science course. Even then, students opt for the courses which they think are "easier," such as botany or geology, rather than chemistry or physics. The result is a scientifically illiterate citizenry, especially as compared to other developed countries.

What are the origins and causes of science anxiety in children? Why are some afflicted and others not? And how can we overcome this fear of learning science so that children may grow up to be, if not professional scientists, then at least technically sophisticated and scientifically literate adults?

Those of us who observe and work with science-anxious students in colleges quickly recognize that the anxiety begins long before that level. Students come to the study of science carrying the emotional baggage of family messages, societal expectations, unhappy school experiences, and media stereotypes of science and scientists. No wonder the Science Anxiety Clinic developed at Chicago's Loyola University is the most popular program offered by the Student Counseling Center.[2] Liberal arts students, pre-meds and pre-nurses, science avoiders, and even science majors seek out the service. Not surprisingly, women constitute the majority of the enrollment in the clinic, since they have learned even more than men to fear and avoid science.

Children receive a number of messages which turn them from natural scientists into science avoiders. The earliest of these begin in the home. It is the rare family that instills a "scientific heritage" in its children. While there

Jeffry V. Mallow, Ph.D., is associate professor of physics at Loyola University of Chicago and the author of Science Anxiety.

are homes where children are taught to love reading or music or art, if parents give their sons and daughters any message at all about science, it is usually "I had a terrible time with this stuff in school!"

The child's second exposure to science is television. There are some outstanding children's TV shows about science. My son David, who is five, has been watching and enjoying "3-2-1 Contact" since he was three. Unfortunately, he has also been watching Saturday morning cartoons, and not a Saturday goes by that he is not exposed to a stereotypical mad scientist cavorting across the screen. So at best, David gets a mixed message: science is sometimes fun, but sometimes it is used by crazy guys in white coats to threaten the world. And since the audience for cartoons swamps the audience for science programs, most children receive a largely negative view of scientists and their work. While it's important not to overemphasize the effect of cartoons on young minds, it has nevertheless been well established by a number of research studies on older children that they view science as an unnatural act. This is mainly due to their stereotypical perceptions of scientists,[3] who are described variously as unfriendly, narrow, withdrawn, highly intelligent but socially inept, and interested in objects rather than people. Such attitudes, coupled with the notion that science is simply too hard for all but a select few, certainly do not encourage children to pursue its study.

Females are in an even worse position than males, because the message to them from family and friends is often quite overt: science is not for girls. Even girls who excel in science (and math) begin to take fewer and fewer courses in those subjects as they get older. Despite a decade of feminist progress, I fear that, for most young girls, being brainy is still considered unfeminine. Furthermore, girls are socialized to believe that women are good at nurturing and communicating and thus skilled in dealing with people. Most women graduating from college, trained in the humanities and service professions—such as nursing and social work—have taken a minimum number of technical courses, and so have been filtered out of interesting and frequently lucrative science-oriented careers.

The child's early experience with science is crucial in shaping attitudes toward the subject. At my son's school, the principal and teachers took parents through an abbreviated day in the kindergarten. One of the subjects offered was science, and a teacher gave us a demonstration about botany. I later asked her, do the students do mostly biology, or do they also do some chemistry and physics? Mostly biology, she said. How often do they study science? I asked. About one hour per week, she answered. And did all the kindergarten teachers divide the task of teaching science among themselves? Well, no. The others were afraid of teaching science, so she did it all.

This pattern repeats itself in schools everywhere. Teachers who themselves fear science and have avoided it in their own education pass these anx-

These puppets help elementary school students learn mathematics in "Math Factory," an instructional television program produced for in-school use by Mississippi ETV and distributed by Great Plains National ITV Television Library.

ieties on to their students. In a typical study done some years ago,[4] it was found that the percentage of high school science teachers who had taken fewer than twenty semester hours (half a major) in their "specialty" was thirteen percent for biology teachers, thirty percent for chemistry teachers, and sixty-three percent for physics teachers!

Science is relegated to a minor role in the elementary school curriculum. Not only is it typically taught for an hour and a half a week, but teachers also tend to schedule it toward the end of the school day, partly out of avoidance, partly because they "run out of time" and can therefore shorten the science session even more. Teachers who fear science cannot mask the fact from their students. Children quickly grasp that adults find the subject difficult and somehow different from all the other subjects. So the natural curiosity of the young becomes stunted by fear.

Science is indeed different from other subjects. For one thing, it requires deductive skills and pattern recognition. Unfortunately, the skill most emphasized in school is memorization. Physics is not simply a list of formulas, nor

"Bread and Butterflies," an instructional series, presents children with examples of successful work behavior and informs them about career opportunities in a number of fields, including oceanography and engineering. *Photo courtesy of Agency for Instructional Television.*

chemistry a list of reactions. Yet many students believe just that, in large measure due to the experiences they have had in school.

There is another type of science teaching that can produce anxiety and aversion. The science teacher who, overtly or covertly, gives the class the message; "I am smarter than you could ever be; you will never grasp this arcane subject as I do" is the Typhoid Mary of science learning. There are enough stereotypes of scientists from other sources without scientists themselves contributing to the problem. The science teacher must be a role model so that students—male and female—can say, "I can be like that, and I might want to!"

The students we work with in the Loyola University Science Anxiety Clinic have had a range of bad science experiences, in and out of the classroom. As a result, they say to themselves, "Science is too hard for normal people" or "I don't have a scientific mind." While we have developed effective techniques for helping them overcome science anxiety, the ideal is to eliminate the causes of this anxiety when they first appear.

There are a number of other causes, in addition to the ones already mentioned. One is the ambivalent attitude of society toward technology. On the one hand, personal computers and video games have become enormously popular, bringing to many a familiarity with, if not an understanding of, modern technological advances. On the other hand, people have become rightfully wary of technologies that may endanger them, such as chemical dumping and nuclear energy. While children might have much to gain from listening to a reasoned discussion of such issues by adults, they gain nothing of value when these discussions degenerate into heated and irrational fights between "good guys" and "bad guys." A five-year-old friend of my son told me that he had gone with his parents to an anti–nuclear rally. What has that taught him about science and technology? Possibly a lot—but only if his parents took the time to explain both sides of the issue to him. Otherwise, he may have come away from the rally with a negative picture of "science" that is not going to help him later in life.

A final cause of science anxiety in young people is the difficulty inherent in teaching science at an appropriate level for different ages. This issue must be faced not only by scientists and science educators, but also by producers and writers of science TV shows for children and teenagers. The root of the difficulty lies in the rate at which children mature intellectually. A child reaching the teens passes through an intellectual transition first described by Swiss psychologist Jean Piaget.[5] The child moves from "concrete-operational" to "formal-operational" thinking. The concrete thinker needs laboratory demonstrations, descriptions of various phenomena—in short, a great deal of "input data." Once this material has been digested, the young person is ready to become a formal thinker, one who can see the patterns behind the data, who can understand theorems and proofs, who can reason "If A, then B, therefore we may conclude C." This transition is supposed to come naturally; however, it occurs at different ages for different children, and apparently it can be helped or hindered by the child's experience with science. Typically seventy-three percent of tenth-graders and fifty percent of college freshmen are concrete-operational.[6] Thus, courses must be geared to both types of students. Obviously, this is difficult: how can we split up a class in high school or college to accommodate everyone's level of thought?

While considerable work is going on at present to design courses that will help move students from concrete to formal thought,[7] the vast majority of science courses in secondary school, and even some in college, are concrete. Furthermore, most science programming on TV is on the level of concrete thought. The simplest way to recognize this is to ask how many science shows focus on the *process* of doing science rather than on the *results* this process has produced.

Admittedly, it is frequently the results that are dramatic: lasers, genetic engineering, space probes. But viewers rarely gain any insight into how scientists decide what problems to attack and how they go about doing it. The outcome of this skewed view is a general impression of science as a powerful and frightening kind of magic. Although the number of high-quality science TV shows has been growing, there is still a lot of progress to be made. Two examples of shows which reached their audiences at precisely the right levels were the concrete "3-2-1 Contact" for young children, and for adults the formal "The Ascent of Man," a series of lectures by Jacob Bronowski.

Children will no longer fear science when their teachers are free of fear. When the messages of the home and of society are "you can understand it"; when gender stereotypes disappear completely from science textbooks and TV shows (including reruns!); and when science is taught and portrayed not just as a series of results, but also as a process, a mode of thought that made those results possible—only then will we see some progress in making science accessible to children.

NOTES

1. J. V. Mallow, *Science Anxiety* (New York: Van Nostrand Reinhold, 1982).

2. S. L. Greenburg and J. V. Mallow, "Treating Science Anxiety at a University Counseling Center," *Journal of Personnel and Guidance* 61 (September 1982): 48–50; J. V. Mallow and S. L. Greenburg, "Science Anxiety: Causes and Remedies," *Journal of College Science Teaching* 11 (1982): 356–358.

3. D. C. Beardslee and D. D. O'Dowd, "The College Student Image of the Scientist," *Science* 133 (1961): 997–1001; L. Hudson, "The Stereotypical Scientist," *Nature* 213 (1967): 228–229.

4. P. W. Tweeten and R. E. Yager, "Content Preparation of Science Teachers in Iowa," *School Science and Mathematics* 68 (1968): 824–833.

5. J. Piaget, *The Psychology of Intelligence* (London: Routledge and Kegan Paul, 1967).

6. J. W. Renner *et al.*, *Research, Teaching, and Learning with the Piaget Model* (Norman, Okla: University of Oklahoma Press, 1976).

7. See, for example, R. G. Fuller, R. Karplus, and A. E. Lawson, "Can Physics Develop Reasoning?" *Physics Today* 30 (February 1978): 23–28.

THE PROBLEM WITH SCIENCE TEACHING

Paul DeHart Hurd

Most descriptions of American culture carry an image of science or technology. "Our time" has been pictured as an atomic age, a space age, and now a computer age. Each of these "ages" is symbolized by a great technical innovation: nuclear power, space probes, the microelectronic chip. Behind these developments is a wealth of basic research in the sciences. This combination of science and technology has made it possible for the United States to become the leading industrial nation in the world. But because the sciences are neglected in all too many school curricula, that status is threatened.

The achievements of science and technology permeate many aspects of American culture, influencing our art, architecture, music, and literature. Science, technology, and the humanities are becoming increasingly connected; few economic, political, or social problems today do not require some understanding of science or technology for a proper interpretation. Yet we find more and more American children growing up foreigners in their own culture, scientifically and technologically illiterate.

One purpose of schooling is to prepare young people to live, work, and participate in their culture. Basic to responsible citizenship and an understanding of the world around us is an understanding of science and technology: the forces of nature, the actions of matter, life's processes, and our own behavior as biological and social organisms. Yet our children are being deprived of this knowledge.

Parents regard learning how to think, reason, and make thoughtful decisions as a primary objective of schooling. The very nature of science as a way of thinking is one reason for including it in the school curriculum, since it helps children develop methods for obtaining and processing information as a means of making judgments and deriving explanations. Careful observation and experimentation are the intellectual tools scientists use for obtaining valid or reliable knowledge. Even first-grade students can learn science through observation and experiment and begin to acquire skills essential to logical thinking. Why, then, is this subject so widely neglected in our schools?

Paul DeHart Hurd, Ed.D., is professor emeritus of education at Stanford University. He has written extensively on science education.

The United States has no national policies for education in technology and the sciences, nor do we have a national curriculum. Instead, we have 17,000 school districts, and with them lies the responsibility for whatever happens in the classroom. Nationwide science tests and national surveys of science teaching in elementary, junior high, and senior high schools verify the problems. These studies reveal a great diversity of schools and teachers, including excellent teachers of science and schools with strong science programs—but not enough of them.

Since colonial days, nature study, or science, has been considered an essential part of the elementary school curriculum. Yet only forty percent of the nation's elementary schools currently require instruction in science. And even in schools where science is mandatory, teachers report that they average twenty minutes per day on science, the smallest amount of time devoted to any major subject. Teachers say they lack time to prepare materials for science classes, especially classes involving experiments and hands-on experiences for children. Does this mean that there is not enough time in the school day to teach children how to think and learn on their own?

Very little assistance is provided to teachers who wish to do a better job of science teaching. Most principals admit they do not feel qualified to help teachers with science. Fewer than a quarter of the country's school districts have a science supervisor or resource person, although only one-fourth of the teachers report that they feel well qualified to teach science. In-service programs are weak and are regarded by teachers as not very useful. A crucial part of revitalizing science education for children, therefore, is correcting the miseducation of teachers.[1]

Getting enough interested and qualified teachers for science subjects at all precollege educational levels is a serious problem. Elementary school teachers, most of whom are women, tend to carry over into their professional lives negative attitudes toward science developed during their childhoods. Both elementary and junior high school science teachers need a broad background in the sciences for the courses they are expected to teach, but their training—if any—is that of a specialist rather than a generalist. Over seventy-five percent of junior high school teachers say they had not planned to teach at this level and have had no preparation for working with early adolescents; junior high science teachers are more dissatisfied with their careers than teachers at any other grade level.[2] The problem in senior high school is also a lack of qualified science teachers, but for somewhat different reasons. Over the past decade there has been a sixty-five percent decline in the number of college students preparing for a science teaching career in the secondary schools. Not only are there not enough qualified science teachers to hire, but twenty-two percent of high school science teachers plan to leave teaching at the first opportunity, largely because they find teaching conditions unacceptable and can make

Snow White beats the witch in a math contest in "It Figures," an instructional television series about math for fourth-graders. *Photo courtesy of Agency for Instructional Television.*

higher incomes in business and industry.[3] None of these problems are easily resolved.

Teaching materials in the science class are also limited. Most teachers depend solely on textbooks and, from time to time, hold discussions. Not many experiments are done, although children like to do experiments best of all. The innovative elementary school science curricula developed with federal funds during the past fifteen years, which include experiments and inquiry activities, have been used in only about thirty percent of all elementary schools, and three-fourths of elementary school teachers say they have never heard of these materials.[4] Almost one-fourth of the schools use a textbook written prior to 1971. In addition, there are nearly fifty commercially published science textbook series available for elementary schools and only one series has managed to capture as much as fifteen percent of the market. This means that while there is considerable overlap in topics included in various textbooks, American children do not obtain a standardized background of common knowledge about science and technology while in elementary school.

The result of our educational system is that more than half of all children complete the sixth grade without ever having had a dedicated science teacher or a well-taught science class. By the end of the third grade, almost half of the children say they would not like to study more science. This attitude continues through junior high school where half the students comment that they do not plan to take more science courses in high school unless they are required. Fewer than one-fifth of the students list science as their favorite subject, although half find it interesting and say they do not mind going to class.[5]

Science teaching in junior high school suffers from many of the same problems found in elementary school. The situation can be considered more crucial, however, since members of this age group (thirteen- to fifteen-year-olds) have begun to think about what they would like to do for their life's work. Studies of outstanding scientists reveal that their interest in science as a career began in the seventh or eighth grade, stimulated by a good teacher or a concerned parent. But with half the students (more girls than boys) "turned off" by science classes before tenth grade, and with two-thirds not confident of their ability to learn science, the nation faces a shortage of well-trained scientists, engineers, and technicians in the future.

Ironically, students at this age like science and believe its results can be used to solve problems by increasing the world's food supply or improving the environment or reducing disease. What they do not like is the way science is taught in school. Students generally feel they have to memorize too many facts and terms. One research team counted the number of technical terms and unfamiliar words in a widely used seventh-grade life science textbook and found 2,500, about twice the vocabulary expected of a student at the same grade level in a foreign language course.[6]

A great deal of what students appear to know about science by age fifteen seems to have been acquired in out-of-school activities: viewing television programs; visiting museums, planetariums, zoos, or science exhibits; participating in junior academies of science, 4-H, or scouting programs; attending summer camp; collecting rocks, flowers, or insects. Regardless of these extracurricular science experiences, national science test scores have declined with each assessment, more so in the physical sciences than in the biological, where the achievement decline seems to have stabilized.

Throughout the world, governments of developed and developing countries recognize an education in science and technology as essential to economic progress and human welfare. To be informed about science and technology is considered a citizen's responsibility, and a person who has a good science education is regarded as a national resource. Instruction in science and technology is viewed as part of the social contract that schools are obligated to fulfill.[7]

A broad look at the educational programs in the U.S.S.R., East Germany, the People's Republic of China, Japan, and West Germany provides clues about how schools go about building scientific and technological literacy. Starting in kindergarten, children attend school 5½ to 6 days a week for 240 days, compared to the U.S.'s 5-day week for 180 days; the school day in the other countries is longer, as well. There are specialized teachers of science from grade four through secondary school. In most of these countries, particularly talented students are encouraged to develop their interests in science. But science is also taught to *all* students, at every grade level, so everyone is exposed to physics, chemistry, earth science, and biology as part of a general education. While these courses meet only two or three days per week, they extend over a period of several years. Students are introduced to the special sciences in the sixth or seventh grade. Specific programs exist to relate science to technical occupations, generally through required work experience in factories or on farms for two weeks to a month each school year. Achievement standards for students are set by an extensive examination system, which is designed to encourage students to compete against the tests' criteria, not against each other. Everyone is expected to pass the examinations, and teachers and students work together to help slower students succeed. Teachers in these countries are expected to carry on a continuing program of self-education and to participate in in-service programs, and scientists and engineers in colleges and universities have a responsibility to help precollege teachers improve science instruction.[8]

Considerable attention is also given in these countries to informal or out-of-school education in the sciences. Newspapers regularly carry science columns, science and technology topics are regularly featured on TV and radio programs, and science and invention books for nonspecialists are numerous and often become best-sellers. There are specialized self-education books designed for teachers or the public. Through all kinds of communication channels, people are made aware of the importance of science and technology and how these fields contribute to the national welfare.

What can be done in the United States to bring about positive changes in science education? First of all, it is essential to create a national awareness of the erosion of science education by alerting parents, school personnel, and local and national government agencies. Parents need to insist that their children be given a balanced education in the natural, physical, and social sciences, as well as the humanities, and that their children be taught by qualified teachers with vision and passion. Colleges and universities must assume more leadership for guiding science education; part of their responsibility must be to identify what is most relevant to the present and future needs of the individual and society. Teacher education in the sciences should be tailored to what teachers are expected to accomplish. They should receive a broader background in the many disciplines and enterprises of science, an understanding of modern concepts of technology, and a knowledge of how both science and technology can contribute to human welfare. Parents have a responsibility to provide a favorable environment for children and to be informed about and supportive of the goals of education. School boards and school administrators need to devote a sizable portion of their time to inspecting the curricula and teaching conditions in their schools.

On a national level we must renew and sustain a commitment to scientific knowledge as our one inexhaustible resource for maintaining a high quality of living and economic well-being. Included in this commitment would be support for basic research and technological innovations, with an endeavor to make both serve the common good. Scientists and engineers have a responsibility to communicate their achievements to nonspecialists so that all may enjoy the intellectual and material results of innovation.

None of these things is likely to happen unless we establish national policies for the pursuit of science and technology, as well as policies for a universal education in the sciences. The coordination of these policies requires a national foundation or academy to focus leadership and to make recommendations about the direction schools should take in reconstructing science courses so as to better serve the individual and promote our national welfare. None of our national science organizations—the American Association for the Advancement of Science, the National Science Foundation, or the National Academy of Sciences, to name several—seems to be filling this role.

Television, as a public communication system, has a responsibility to improve scientific and technological literacy. Television science programs for young people can start by trying to answer their audience's questions. Children are curious about plants, animals, people, natural phenomena, and innovations in technology such as space probes, microcomputers, and robots. Young adolescents want to know what scientists, professional engineers, and technical workers do. By demonstrating experiments that children can easily duplicate at home, by showing classrooms where children are engaged in innovative and interesting science activities, or by featuring topics that children are naturally excited by, television programs could encourage young people to pursue scientific inquiry on their own. Programming like this would not only inform and entertain young viewers but also suggest to parents and teachers ways to help children learn science.

Ideally, broadcasters should be active members of the coalition of representatives of business, industry, government, science, engineering, and education, all of whom are seeking to revitalize science education in the U.S. Together, we can help to insure the scientific and technological intellectual capital of this nation, and make it possible for people to live more interesting lives.

NOTES

1. R. E. Stake and J. Easley, *Case Studies in Science Education*, vol. 2. (Washington, D.C.: Government Printing Office, 1978).

2. P. DeH. Hurd, J. T. Robinson, M. C. McConnell, and N. M. Ross, Jr., *The Status of Middle School and Junior High School Science*, 2 vols. (Louisville, Colo.: Center for Educational Research and Evaluation, 1981).

3. Information cited in the testimony to the Committee on Labor and Human Resources of the U.S. Senate by the National Science Teachers Association on April 15, 1982.

4. I. R. Weiss, *Report of the 1977 National Survey of Science, Mathematics and Social Studies Education* (Washington, D.C.: Government Printing Office, 1977).

5. Hurd *et al., Status*, vol. 1.

6. *Ibid.*

7. P. DeH. Hurd, "State of Precollege Education in Mathematics and Science," *Science Education* 67 (1983): 57–67.

8. National Academy of Sciences, *Science and Mathematics Education in the Schools: Report of a Convocation* (Washington, D.C.: National Academy Press, 1982): 4–5.

SCIENCE OUTSIDE
THE CLASSROOM

The sciences are of a sociable disposition, and flourish best in the neighborhood of each other; nor is there any branch of learning but may be helped and improved by assistance drawn from the other arts.

Sir William Blackstone, *jurist*
(1723–1780)

The ways in which children can be introduced to science undoubtedly go beyond the classroom, the family, and the TV set. These other exposures to science, whether incidental or intentional, may become special moments when a particular chord of curiosity is struck: a spark that starts the child's interest in a whole new field.

In the first essay of this chapter, Steven Marcus, technology editor at the *New York Times*, writes about how science has fared in the movies, from the Flash Gordon serials of the 1940s to *E.T.*

Books and magazines do not have the instant, nationwide impact of movies and television, but they do influence children's thinking about science. Boyce Rensberger, former head writer for the children's science series "3-2-1 Contact" and now senior editor at *Science 84*, has written about science books for children: how adults choose them and what sometimes causes them to choose badly.

Frank Oppenheimer, director, and Robert Semper, associate director of the Exploratorium in San Francisco, talk about the joint educational strengths of science museums and television. Wally Longul, a TVOntario executive producer responsible for "Fast Forward," closes with a speculation on children's exposure to computers and videodiscs as educational tools.

HUMANIZING DOCTOR ZARKOV

Steven J. Marcus

Flash Gordon had a scientist sidekick, Dr. Zarkov, who was one smart guy. In their movie serials of the 1940s, which I later watched on television when I was a boy in the 1950s, I was continually amazed by what that learned man could do. He'd routinely explain the most bizarre phenomenon, devise the cleverest escape, construct the most exotic machine—often at a moment's notice. The topper for me came during one episode that called for Flash and Zarkov to go back in time—several centuries' worth—to our own era. The writers must have thought it would be neat for these futuristic characters to see and comment on "modern" America. Good old Zarkov whipped up a time-travel machine in a single afternoon.

I can't recall the children's program on which I saw this particular episode, but it had a "peanut gallery," a group of on-camera kiddies seated around the grown-up host. Usually the host would go right to the next segment of the show or a commercial after the "Flash Gordon" episode. But he too was impressed with this particular piece of scientific virtuosity, because he felt obliged to stop and comment, "Dr. Zarkov could do this, boys and girls, because he went to school, studied hard, and did his homework."

I, too, went to school (and on to engineering school), studied hard, and did my homework. But despite the many problem sets I conquered, the grades I achieved, and the degrees I earned, I still cannot invent a time machine at all, much less in a single afternoon. It could well be that I didn't choose my courses as wisely as Zarkov did, but I've begun to suspect that his skills and accomplishments were slightly exaggerated. His creators, and that kiddie show host, sure gave me a bum steer.

The common characteristic of most scientists in the movies—what makes them so unlike real people—is their one-dimensionality. In my fifties fantasies, for example, I liked to think that Zarkov—when he'd take a break from being uniformly brilliant—was basically a good guy. I could see him voting for Adlai Stevenson, digging Elvis, and chuckling at *MAD* magazine. But I really couldn't know any of that from his on-screen personality, which was nil. I don't believe he even had a first name, unless it was Doctor. The man

Steven J. Marcus, Ph.D., is technology editor at the New York Times.

The movie *E.T. The Extra Terrestrial*, with its loving children and frightening—but ineffectual—scientists, created something of a controversy: some have claimed that the movie is anti-science, while others have defended it. *Photo courtesy of MCA Publishing, a Division of MCA Communications, Inc. Copyright © by Universal Pictures, a Division of Universal City Studios, Inc.*

was an achievement machine—a "brain"—not a believable human being. That kind of stereotyped scientist is a Hollywood standby; anyone who seems to have access to the secrets of the universe gets portrayed as one-dimensional in the extreme. So movie scientists are usually either maniacs or milquetoasts, virtuosos or bunglers, saintly good or diabolically evil.

Sometimes they are intent on ruling the world, or at least a goodly part of it. In *Dr. No*, the arch-adversary of James Bond intends to trigger a nuclear war between the superpowers through some very high technology tricks, and emerge influential when their mutual destruction is complete. Lex Luthor, nemesis in the *Superman* movies, forever concocts ultrasophisticated plans for world conquest that only a superman can (just barely) foil. The unscrupulous surgeon in *The Black Sleep* (a fifties thriller) disfigures and denatures one person after another in his relentless quest to master the human brain. A whole network of unscrupulous surgeons in *Coma* operate a lucrative multinational business in spare body parts involuntarily donated by their ex-patients. We do not know why these scientists are so driven, how they manage to live with their grand illusions, or how they expect to get away with their various outrageous schemes. These guys are not people, however. They are power machines. ("Knowledge is power." Get it?)

Of course, that mythic power can be used in the opposite direction, and therein lies another time-honored stereotype: the impossibly wonderful sage. In the monster movies of the fifties, for example, there is no technological threat, whether alien (death rays hurled at us from another planet) or earthly (giant ants crazed by atomic testing) that some kindly old scientist, teaming up with a square-jawed air force general, cannot neutralize by the last reel. Back in the forties, Claude Raines, an incredibly knowledgeable, gentle, yet modest psychiatrist in *Now, Voyager*, brought problem-ridden Bette Davis back into society. Judd Hirsch, playing a modern variation on the same theme in *Ordinary People*, performs a similar service for Timothy Hutton. No impediment conceived by man, woman, or God can stop archaeologist/adventurer Harrison Ford in *Raiders of the Lost Ark*; the fellow knows and can do everything. Superprogrammer Jeff Bridges in *Tron* is invincible in the world of computers—literally within them and without them. It is fun to watch these larger-than-life (or, in the latter case, microscopically-smaller-than-life) characters outthink opponents and conquer problems that would defeat the average human within seconds. But it also contributes to a set of highly unrealistic expectations about what actual scientists can and cannot do.

At the other end of the spectrum from "science will save us" is the increasingly popular movie theme of "science will do us in." This usually features not the scientist per se, but his or her misbegotten creations. The omniscient computer HAL in *2001: A Space Odyssey* decides to eliminate the flawed human element. Arcane technologies like nuclear power plants, as depicted in *The China Syndrome*, threaten society both directly with their environmental risks and indirectly through their apparent ability to bring out the worst in just about everyone. In *Futureworld*, we find that even Walt-Disney-like robots can turn against us. In *The Stepford Wives*, the women of a Connecticut town (whose local industry is aerospace) are systematically replaced by docile look-alike robots. (Why? Explains the engineer in charge: "Because we know how.") In *Fail Safe*, a malfunctioning nuclear weapons system brings about the destruction of Moscow and New York; in *On the Beach* and *Dr. Strangelove*, the whole world goes down the drain.

Have the movies gone from awe to anger with respect to scientists and their handiwork? Is *either* extreme desirable? A healthier tendency, it seems to me, is to stake out a more neutral position: science will help save us in one situation and hurt us in another, depending on the wisdom of those in charge, but often it is not the critical factor at all. Science cannot identify the problem nor help to solve it in *The Exorcist*; ironically, it is religion that has the insights. In *The Day the Earth Stood Still*, we don't have the sense to recognize a good thing from outer space when we see one. In the remake of *Invasion of the Body Snatchers*, our science—and all other knowledge—is pathetically ineffectual as a bad thing from outer space takes over completely. In *E.T.*, human scientists give up on the alien, having neither the knowledge of what makes him tick nor the skill to revive him. High-tech hullabaloo is everywhere in the three *Star Wars* movies, but without some semi-mystical knowledge of The Force it's all a pile of junk. In an early but fascinating epic, *Forbidden Planet*, a highly advanced civilization appears to have done itself in—despite the greatness of its rational science—because it forgot about the unconscious mind and its "monsters from the id."

In many of the above examples, especially the more recent, scientists are shown as intolerant, petulant, selfish, and of limited competence. Are these films "anti-science?" Director Steven Spielberg, in films such as *Jaws*, *Close Encounters of the Third Kind*, and *E.T.*, depicts scientists as all too human in their imperfections. Is Spielberg anti-science? Columnist George F. Will certainly thinks so. In *E.T.*, he says, science is presented as a "spoilsome intrusion" in nature's sweet garden, "as a morbid calling for callous vivisectionists and unfeeling technocrats." I must admit I had a similar initial response to the scientists in *Close Encounters*: they kept getting in the way of the fun. What right did those guys have, anyway, to "protect" the public from the spectacular and historic landing of the Mother Ship?

Yet I don't think that Spielberg or his colleagues are anti-science. The children in *E.T.* are comfortable in matters technological. The extraterrestrial's escape is made possible not by some Zarkovian fantasy but by his rigging of a transmitter from the children's own toys and household items. He is a "higher intelligence" but he is also, if you'll pardon the expression, down-to-earth. The spaceship itself, despite the awesome capabilities it must surely possess, appears warm and slightly eccentric—even a little Victorian. This is technology with charm and feeling, which to me is not anti-science at all but its opposite.

E.T. and similar films might appear anti-science because scientists are a prominent subset of the writers' main target: grown-up authority figures. And all grown-ups, whether they are scientists or not, can be ignorant and foolish.

Adults are sometimes less than observant of what may be lying all around them and have been known to act on superficial evidence. More often than not, they don't stop to consider the alternatives, or The Big Picture, or their own feelings. Given the powerful tools at their disposal, the results are often harmful on a large scale.

I'm very pleased about such depictions of scientists because they resemble real people—no smarter or more capable than any other class of humans. It's a reminder that one particular kind of knowledge, regardless of how interesting and powerful it may be, needs other, complementary kinds of knowledge to be truly enlightened and effective. Ironically, the portrayal of an occasionally shortsighted or bungling scientist is a more positive image for children, it seems to me, than one of an all-knowing worker of miracles. It is a more accurate picture of adults as children see them and as they really are. And it doesn't diminish the prestige of science, which most audiences—grown or growing—take as given. In fact, it makes science seem more human and accessible, which is the way it is and should appear.

Another reason films with scientists as main characters may appear anti-science is that screenwriters generally do poorly at portraying *any* particular occupation realistically. Not knowing the field they are depicting, they tend to exaggerate or trivialize, and the characters appear as extreme types. If businesspeople really made deals the way they are shown in most films, there'd either be no reason why almost anyone couldn't be a millionaire, or else it would be virtually impossible for anyone to make a dime. If novelists worked at their typewriters the way we see them on the screen, we'd either all be autographing each other's books or else we'd have no fiction to read whatsoever. If real reporters performed their jobs the way movie reporters do, reading the newspaper could be the most—or least—transcendent experience in our lives. Screenwriters are a lot better at depicting more universal situations; specific ones often elude them. But they're learning more about science and technology, along with everyone else, and their screenplays are fast becoming more sophisticated.

Such sophistication is evident even in "grim future" pictures like *Blade Runner* and *Outland*. Science provides fascinating scenes and visual effects and is an integral part of the story, but the reason for the grimness is not necessarily scientific. It is the usual set of personal, moral, social, political, and economic dilemmas that pervade all human endeavor, in life as well as art. Giving science a bigger part doesn't make it the cause of the conflict.

As science becomes more and more accessible to the public at large, its influence will continue to grow in Hollywood, not only in the story on the screen but in the techniques which place it there. And as filmmaking becomes an increasingly high-tech business, the scientific insights of the filmmakers will grow accordingly. But although we can expect science to have a more

81

realistic role in film, it would be unrealistic for the audience to think that it is seeing science as it really is. For one thing, film is a visual medium, but many of the scientific issues we'd hope to see developed are subtle and not very obvious. For another, movies have time constraints: the problem must be presented, confronted, and resolved in 120 minutes or less, and that is not the way of the real world. Research and development proceed slowly, as do their benefits and solutions to the side effects they have been known to cause. When the story seems superficial, dealing mostly with the tip of the iceberg, sometimes the culprit is not the studio but the size and complexity of the iceberg.

As long as filmmakers do the minimum amount of homework in depicting science and scientists, so that what eventually appears isn't defeating the story line or the believability of the characters, realism is not the primary goal. A more appropriate and practical goal is to inject some creativity into the portrayal of technology. Movie theaters have often been called "houses built for dreams." And although scientists and engineers may help to fulfill human dreams, it is really up to our tellers of tales and singers of songs and sayers of sooth to continually challenge and shock us with the visions that dreams are made of. If the scientist and the filmmaker continue to inspire each other, the future may not be so grim after all.

SCIENCE ON THE CHILDREN'S SHELVES

Boyce Rensberger

Parents who shop in a general-purpose bookstore, looking for science books for their children, are unlikely to see many of the better titles available. Most bookstores simply don't stock them. You have to go to a shop that specializes in children's books (there are said to be only about forty in the country that do this exclusively) or to a library with an experienced children's librarian.

People who are unaware of this dual marketplace phenomenon may have a lopsided impression of trends in science books for children. Depending on which marketplace they are more familiar with, book seekers tend to conclude either that the field is doing well, responsibly publishing a large number of high-quality reading materials for children, or that the field is doing badly, cynically churning out mass-appeal books almost bereft of good taste, respect for children's minds, or regard for the value of accuracy.

In both marketplaces, however, it appears that science books for children are being produced in abundance. Moreover, people in and around the industry say the volume has been strong for a number of years. I estimate, from my interviews with buyers for children's bookstores and study of book reviews, that about two hundred (plus or minus fifty) new books a year are aimed specifically at the children's science market. Their titles are often explicit: *Frozen Earth: Explaining the Ice Ages* or *Silicon Chips and You.* Perhaps an equal number convey "scientific information" but embed it in such a "non-scientific" form that most people wouldn't readily think of the book as science. The titles of these covert science books sound more like entertainment: *Snoopy's Facts and Fun Book about Seashores,* where a few natural history facts are sprinkled through a plotless "story" for preschoolers, or *Einstein Anderson Shocks His Friends,* part of an excellent fiction series for the middle primary grades written by a former science teacher who also does overt science books.

There are indications that the quality of a number of the books published each year is high and steadily improving. Certainly there are more ex-

Boyce Rensberger is senior editor of Science 84 *and was head writer for "3-2-1 Contact" during its first season.*

The Einstein Anderson books turn science into a series of mysteries which only their young hero can solve. Here he tries out his friend Stanley's "automatic fitting machine." Illustration by Fred Winkowski from *Einstein Anderson: Science Sleuth* by Seymour Simon. *Illustration copyright © 1980 by Viking Penguin, Inc. Reprinted with permission of Viking Penguin, Inc.*

citing books available than a parent could afford to buy. This is another reason why a good public library is an especially important resource. My impressions are confirmed by Zena Sutherland, a respected authority on children's books, who wrote in a recent issue of *American Libraries* magazine that today's science titles are better written, cover a broader range of subjects, and are more scientifically reliable than ever. Opinions gathered informally from others in and around the field support this view. Nevertheless, there are still plenty of terrible books purporting to be about science that also find their way onto bookshelves in libraries and shops.

One important question is whether buyers can tell the good books from the bad. An answer that makes sense to me emerges from an analysis of the dual marketplace phenomenon, which exists because children do not select or purchase science books for themselves; adults do it for them. Thus, just as the makers of baby food used to put so much sugar and salt into their products to satisfy adult tastes, children's books are made to appeal to adults. In the science category, this means that the books try to offer what adults think is good for children and not necessarily what children like.

There are two groups of adults who do most of the buying—parents and librarians—and there are significant differences in what they think is good for children, as reflected in the way they select books. If a book is going to sell well, it must either be made appealing to parents—most of whom are unfamiliar with science and often uncomfortable about it—or to librarians—most of whom are also unfamiliar and uncomfortable with science but who are trained to heed the recommendations of credentialed scientists in one or more of the publications that review science books for children. Both groups look for qualities in a book that appeal to their conceptions of what science is.

An adult—parent or librarian—who thinks science is a vast accumulation of facts about animals or atoms or anything else is going to buy books crammed with, as the jackets say, "amazing" or "astounding" facts. These books have no story in the sense of a narrative with a beginning, middle, and end. They are essentially grab bags of facts linked only in that they all pertain to some subject—meat-eaters, for example, or astronomy or insects. These are books for browsing. Titles of books that appeal to this mentality often include words such as "All About . . ." or "Wonders of . . .". This is by far the most common kind of science book available. I would guess that well over half the titles on the shelves of ordinary bookstores are of this category. Children's libraries have quite a few of these, too.

While every good scientist does, of course, accumulate a considerable body of facts, science is much more than this. It is a process of creating those facts by observing and experimenting and trying to describe what has been found out. If all we want out of science education is to cram lots of facts into kids' heads, maybe the grab bag books are okay. But if we want science education to inculcate children with a certain intellectual style as well (the intellectual style they need to be more than sheep in today's world), then we must look for something more in the science books children read.

Science is also a process of questioning and, perhaps, destroying "facts," an ongoing re-evaluation of "the truth." An adult who fails to grasp the perpetually revisionist tendency of science is not necessarily going to select books that really get science across as the kind of activity it is. This misunderstanding is common among nonscientists and seems to guide the book buying of most parents. While librarians often suffer from the same misconceptions of science that afflict parents, many are saved from unwise book purchases by their practice of checking first with one or more of the better journals that review books for librarians.

As it happens, there is one periodical devoted exclusively to children's science books. It is called *Appraisal: Science Books for Young People*, and is published three times a year by the Children's Science Book Review Committee, a nonprofit organization sponsored by the New England Roundtable of Children's Librarians and the Department of Science and Mathematics Education at Boston University School of Education. I cite it at such length because it is probably the most useful single aid available to any adult who is serious about selecting science books for children. Each issue reviews fifty to ninety new books, offering two appraisals of each, one by a children's librarian and one by a scientist specializing in the book's subject. Each reviewer also rates the book on a five-point scale.

Science Books & Films, published five times a year by the American Association for the Advancement of Science, also reviews children's books—about thirty in a typical issue, along with some three hundred books for adults. Reviewers may be scientists, librarians, teachers, or others with related expertise. The shortest but by far the most literate reviews of children's science books, however, can be found every December in *Scientific American*, to which Philip Morrison, the distinguished MIT physicist, and his wife, Phylis, contribute twenty to thirty reviews. In addition, established reviewing journals, such as *School Library Journal, The Horn Book,* and *Booklist* all include regular reviews of science books for children.

Although some of the reviewing journals are shoestring operations, their mere existence is a sign that the field of children's science books is more mature than that of, say, children's science television. Other signs of established good health in the field include the fact that children's science books are also reviewed and otherwise discussed in magazines such as *School Science and Mathematics, The School Science Review, Science Education, Science and Children,* and *The Science Teacher.* Also, excellence in the field is encouraged by two annual awards offered by the New York Academy of Sciences and one offered by the American Nature Society.

Because they rely on responsible reviews, librarians are more likely than parents browsing in a bookstore to buy science books that pass muster with the scientific community. Sometimes, drab and dull books—volumes that most children would ignore and most booksellers never stock—wind up on a library shelf simply because they were technically accurate enough to win a good rating from a scientific reviewer. But generally librarans take into consideration both appeal to children and quality of coverage when they select books.

Despite the activity within the field of children's science books, there are still not very many science books that a child will choose to read for pleasure, especially when the child has free choice of activities. With science being taught so poorly in most schools and almost not at all on children's television, one might hope that books could fill the gap. But the only books that could do this would be those a child would enjoy on his or her own.

I am not thinking here of children who are good readers or who develop a burning curiosity about a subject. Under these special conditions, strongly motivated kids will plunge through all sorts of obstacles to get what they want. I'm concerned about the vast majority of kids, who are rarely turned on to science or whose interest is limited to a science project assignment. It's unlikely that these young people will freely select a book on the physical chemistry of clouds or the lives of spiders, no matter how good a rating it has received from a scientist reviewing the book for a library journal. These may be among the better books available in terms of accuracy, taste, and even clarity of writing, but that does not mean they are among the most appealing to most children. As a matter of fact, these traditional books are often not even appealing to kids who really do like science. I live with an eleven-year-old whose grasp of scientific matters repeatedly astonishes me, and I have had a hard time getting him to read even the best of the nonfiction science books I have examined.

For many children, reading is enough of a chore that the effort of getting through any nonfiction book, no matter how fascinating or well-written, may be considered punitive, not rewarding. Advocates of the list-of-facts type of book argue that short snippets of text are easier on poor readers than long narratives. I would agree, if one ignores the matter of motivation. But since motivation is probably the biggest factor to worry about in both reading education and science education, I would argue that a good narrative, with effective character development and a fast-moving plot, will motivate almost any reader to keep reading far beyond the point at which the snippet approach fails.

This might seem a tall order but, in fact, there is a small body of books that seems to do this. These are the books the publishers would all be publishing if children, not adults, bought science books. They are part of what I have called the covert science book category, and the best example I know of is the *Einstein Anderson* series. Written by Seymour Simon, the books are fictional accounts of a bright young boy who uses logic, scientific knowledge, and the scientific method (although it is rarely called that) to solve various mysteries that he and his school-age friends encounter. This series holds up the intellectual style of science that is seldom conveyed by the list-of-facts books. Somewhat similar is the *Encyclopedia Brown* series by Donald J. Sobol. In this series, the hero is the son of a small town police chief who cracks forensic mysteries that stump his dad. The *Encyclopedia Brown* books are less "sciency" than the *Einstein Anderson* series but still strong on logic and systematic problem solving. Older examples of the good use of fiction in science (not, please, science fiction) include Jean George's 1972 book, *Julie of the*

Wolves, which teaches wolf biology, and her *Spring Comes to the Ocean*, published in 1965. Like Simon, George also writes very good nonfiction science books.

In addition to books, there are a few periodicals dealing with science that are published for children. There is a *3-2-1 Contact* magazine, published by Children's Television Workshop, but it is, in my opinion, a lightweight effort, concerned more with razzle-dazzle pages than with science. National Geographic publishes *World*, but aside from one or two soft animal picture stories, it has little science. Even more animal-oriented, but somewhat stronger on the science, is *Ranger Rick's Nature Magazine*, published by the National Wildlife Federation. Recently, a few new magazines for children have been attempted—I am aware of ones specializing in astronomy and computers—but their quality is not impressive and they are definitely for the child who already has a strong interest in a science specialty. As far as I know, there is nothing in the science field to compare to the quality of an excellent children's magazine, *Cricket*, which does occasionally run science pieces.

This lack of science magazines for children stands in contrast to the recent flowering of science and technology magazines for adults. Some teachers do, of course, make use of articles in *Science 84*, *Discover*, and *Science Digest*. And, I suspect, some children have picked up and at least looked at copies belonging to their parents. It is tempting to suggest that the market seems right for a strong children's science magazine devoted not to a specialty interest but to the natural interests of children—animals, everyday phenomena, etc.—and with a good dose of science-based fiction.

My faith in the power of fiction to hold children's attention is supported by what I learned working on "3-2-1 Contact," a Children's Television Workshop production that remains one of the few major efforts in the television industry to present science to children. The show consists of about eight percent factual presentation and twenty percent tightly scripted fiction having to do with a group of youngsters who run a detective agency and solve crimes, a concept borrowed from *Encyclopedia Brown*. Test screenings before groups of school children showed that the fiction usually kept young viewers far more interested than the other portions.

Unfortunately, these segments on "3-2-1 Contact," called "The Bloodhound Gang," contain precious little science. Yet I see no reason why a new TV series with a little more science in it wouldn't be as interesting to kids. In fact, if I were a producer wanting to do a new TV series for children, I'd try to recruit Seymour Simon to write *Einstein Anderson* teleplays or to collaborate with a teleplay writer. I suspect that for every hundred children who watched this proposed fictional science series and learned only ten units of science, a factual presentation or "Mr. Wizard" approach would reverse the proportions, getting a hundred units of science into only ten of the children. Both types of presentations have an important educational role to play, on TV or in writing.

Further evidence of the importance of fiction as a teaching tool can be found in the popularity of Dungeons and Dragons, the role-playing game in which youngsters create fictional characters with various realistic and magical attributes and then "control" them. Grouped with other playmate-controlled creations, the characters go adventuring, meeting dragons and other monsters, usually in a medieval setting resembling the Middle-earth world of J.R.R. Tolkien. Once hooked on the game, D&D aficionados are apt to spend their allowances on various books, manuals, guides, and other paraphernalia used to make the game more complex. You don't "win" at D&D; you play for the sake of playing. But it is a game nonetheless and, I am certain, the most complicated game ever devised. My eleven-year-old spends at least half his reading time poring over D&D books and magazines. His mother and I used to worry that it was a passion more consuming and more insidious than video games.

Yet I have come to a new appreciation of Dungeons and Dragons, especially after talking with parents of other D&D addicts. First of all, it is one of the most powerful motivations for children to read that I know of. Several parents have told me their child's vocabulary, especially for various medieval objects and concepts, has soared. More useful, however, is the intellectual training that occurs as a child seeks to master a most complex game. Playing it well requires an ability to remember a set of facts at least as complex as the metabolic pathways of living organisms or the interactions of many kinds of subatomic particles. A child who plays D&D becomes familiar with situations in which many variables act and interact simultaneously. If an important purpose of school is to teach children how to learn, then D&D does that, at least for the kinds of complex, multivariable situations that scientists encounter all the time. D&D does lack any place for controlled experimentation and one or two other essentials of a good science education, so it cannot substitute entirely for school.

Now if somebody could only devise a science text that arranged the roles of the chemical elements—with their various attributes and abilities to interact—as if they were D&D characters and monsters ... or give the roles of DNA, gene-repressors, ribosomes, and the other entities of molecular biology as much panache as the writers of D&D manuals give their characters ... or animate a Dungeons and Dragons lesson in astronomy for children's television ...!

SCIENCE MUSEUMS AND TV: THE PERFECT MATCH

Frank Oppenheimer and Robert J. Semper

Developing a scientific understanding of nature is a multifaceted endeavor. Skills in observation, problem solving, analysis, mathematics, logic, experimentation, and synthesis are all ultimately essential. Given this variety of activities, it is not surprising that media as different as schools, books, television, films, magazines, zoos, and museums can each provide different and complementary elements of science education. It is instructive, therefore, to examine each of these media with a view toward determining which elements of science learning they can best supply. Here we concentrate on science museums, television, and the ways that cooperation between them can produce a better educated public.

Throughout the United States, there are over eight hundred public science institutions, including zoos, aquariums, natural science parks, planetariums, natural history museums, and science centers.[1] Each of these facilities has exhibits and programs that present science to children and adults using objects and experiences. These institutions reach a large cross section of the population. In 1979, over 34 million visits were made to science centers alone.

Public science centers have a number of attributes that make them both popular and useful as part of the science education process. First and foremost, in a museum setting visitors are in control of the pace, style, and even the subject matter of their learning. Unlike schools, museums do not require attendance; where visitors go and what exhibits they choose to explore depend on their own curiosity and interest. There are few constraints on how long one spends at a particular exhibit or which topic one studies. In addition, the questions asked and the answers received by a museum visitor are his or her own and not those of a teacher or course syllabus. Many exhibits have elements that can be manipulated and altered to give the important "What will happen if . . .?" experience essential for deep understanding. Museums provide an opportunity for education that is both personal and appropriate for the individual learner in a way that standardized instruction cannot hope

Frank Oppenheimer, Ph.D., is founder and director of the Exploratorium and professor emeritus of physics at the University of Colorado.
Robert J. Semper, Ph.D., is a physicist who is associate director of the Exploratorium.

to be. Because of the diversity of the exhibits, the education a museum offers fits the background, training, ability, and interest of the visitor—and all without the evaluative pressure of a class. No one has ever flunked a museum!

Museums can also provide a rich overview of a topic by virtue of the number of exhibits and objects they contain. As a visitor goes from one exhibit to another, his or her own interests create a unity between the assortment of materials on display. By combining exhibits with demonstrations, pictures, films, and works of art, museums provide an important opportunity for supportive social interaction during the learning process. Visitors are encouraged to teach each other about the things that excite them. At the San Francisco Exploratorium, for example, students who have been to the museum on class field trips bring their families back on the weekend for a repeat visit, and we often see parents teaching their children or children teaching their parents things they have discovered.

Museums also provide access to the "real thing," whether it be a historical object like Edison's original apparatus, or natural phenomena, such as the refraction of light or the display posture of animals. The "real thing" always has a richer complexion than a diagram or model and therefore allows experimentation in many different ways, including some that are surprising even to the exhibit builder. The museum experience can awaken or reawaken a curiosity about nature that motivates further study and questioning. Since, at its most fundamental level, science is the ordered study of nature, direct experience with the natural world is a vital element in all of science education.

But museums can only perform part of the science education task. Because of their informal nature, they rarely do well at teaching such skills as mathematical computation or problem solving (although classes taught at museums using the exhibits can sometimes do this). It is possible to create a museum "curriculum" by providing a number of exhibits on similar topics, but the integration of ideas is still best accomplished by classroom instruction and books. Some natural processes have time frames that make direct observation quite difficult. Visitors to zoos or aquariums, for example, often miss the slow process of animal growth and development, which can be better shown on film.

Other aspects of science, such as quantum mechanics or the theory of evolution, are exceedingly hard to visualize or exhibit and are best presented with books. Finally, museums are hard-pressed to present social or economic issues in as exciting and useful a way as they do objects or phenomena. It is hard to provide a self-discovery experience relating to these topics, and most museums are reduced to using written descriptions or stage sets to cover socioeconomic material. In most cases, providing exposure to these issues can be much better done through books, classroom discussions, or television documentaries. (The integration of social, economic, and technical ideas has,

Visitors at the Exploratorium in San Francisco watch the dissection of a cow's eye. *Photo by Nancy Rodger, courtesy of the Exploratorium. Copyright © 1980 by Nancy Rodger.*

however, been successfully presented in "living" museums, such as Colonial Williamsburg, that show historical technology in action in a community setting.)

An important aspect of education is sightseeing: that is, seeing what is around and investigating that which attracts one's interest. Museums and science centers provide a rich environment for this activity. But television offers a form of vicarious sightseeing that leads viewers to places and sights almost impossible to visit in person. Programs like "The Undersea World of Jacques Cousteau" or the "National Geographic Specials" can take a viewer to distant lands or to the worlds of the atom and the stars at an unbelievably low cost per viewer. This enlargement of the viewer's world provides excitement and stimulation that is hard to duplicate. The medium is also best when involving viewers with immediate, unfolding events—the eruption of Mount St. Helens or the launching of a lunar mission—so that millions of viewers have a sense of being there in person. Television can *show* exactly what is happening as well as talk about it, a remarkable capability that TV producers sometimes fail to take advantage of. Philip Morrison, Institute Professor at MIT and a creator of wonderfully rich science television, has remarked, "The key thing in a science film is to show the evidence."[2]

Film and television can also effectively portray the process of science and the human element of scientific endeavor, whether it be through historical programs such as the PBS/BCC series on Madame Curie or current documentaries like "NOVA" or "The Search for Solutions." In programs like Children's Television Workshop's "3-2-1 Contact," scientists provide role models for children, encouraging them to consider science as a future career.

Television's need for an audience influences its treatment of science. It is important to note that much of the science education that happens through this medium occurs in programming that would not normally be considered scientific or educational. Weather broadcasts, for example, offer science to a large population every night, and science is even presented—although in a distorted fashion—in commercials.

But the big problem with any educational use of television is time, or, more precisely, the lack of control over time. Everyone's pace of understanding varies, yet it is impossible to stop a broadcast and wait while someone catches up. This makes television presentations of complex concepts especially hard. The flood of uncontrollable images onto the TV screen also tends to generate a passivity in the viewer that suffocates the questioning and examination necessary for education. In this respect, radio allows for more active audience participation because of its ability to challenge the mind to build its own images and patterns in response to the presentation of a specific concept. The excellent science reports on National Public Radio's "All Things Considered" are a good example of this.

In an attempt to create an artificial excitement and hold viewers' interest, TV pieces are often cut at a rapid pace, and they address a number of different topics during a single program. This leads to a fragmented and incomplete educational experience. And although the use of scientist-personalities such as Carl Sagan and David Attenborough provides an essential personal connection between the home viewer and difficult intellectual material, science "hosts" *can* foster an authoritarian view of science, reinforcing the belief that science is a collective set of right answers.

Given all of these various attributes of museums and television, it becomes apparent that only through the combination of these media can truly exciting science education occur. For example, museums by their very nature provide strong visual stimuli. Since television—especially science television—has a continuing need for visual material, museums can be a ready source of TV settings. At a 1981 conference on Science Media held at the Exploratorium,[3] Jon Ward, producer of the CBS series "Universe," suggested that museums should create a directory of exhibits and objects that lend themselves to being filmed for television. This would be of great help to TV producers, in a similar manner to the American Association for the Advancement of Science's list of locations where specific scientific research is underway.

The interconnection of television and museums can be carried one step further by using exhibits for the presentation of a particular idea or phenomenon. For example, a number of brief segments were taped at the Exploratorium to answer questions about the weather that had been sent in by viewers to a local television station. These included the old standby, "Why is the sky blue?", as well as questions like "Why do winds circulate around a low pressure area?". Existing exhibits and newly constructed demonstrations were used to provide the answers. The segments were then inserted into the nightly weather broadcasts.

Sometimes museums themselves can serve as the originators of TV programming. The Exploratorium is currently developing a TV series on natural phenomena—shadows, waves, randomness—that will combine the use of museum exhibits with outdoor film footage and discussions of art and literature. One of the important by-products of TV programs like these (and of any TV show featuring a museum) is that TV viewers are encouraged to visit the exhibits they have seen on the screen. Finally, one of the best resources that science museums can offer producers of science programming is the museum staff itself. Like TV producers, museum people are familiar with the problems of attracting an audience. Museums' staff members teach the general public every day, and they have substantial information about how much people understand and what can be done to help them understand better. It might not be a bad idea for producers to try out new programming ideas on a science museum staff, as a test of audience reaction.

These are only some of the ways that museums and television can work together; other examples abound. Television programs that sketch historical and geographical background for major museum shows such as the "King Tut" exhibition add a level of richness that the museum cannot provide alone. Or a series like Jacob Bronowski's "The Ascent of Man" can provide both historical and an intellectual context for a variety of exhibits. A special exhibit can be mounted in association with a particular broadcast, or a TV program can refer viewers to a museum exhibition offering more detailed explanations of program content. It is also possible for a museum (or a library or school, for that matter) to sponsor a second viewing of a program like "NOVA," followed by a discussion with a local scientist.

Carrying this kind of coordination one step further, the ideal science education experience would include elements from a number of different media. For example, a television special on genetic engineering, featuring interviews with scientists and visits to their laboratories, could be broadcast to coincide with a newspaper series describing gene splicing in greater detail and illustrating it with diagrams that take more time for a reader to absorb. A local museum might, at the same time, build exhibits on DNA and gene splicing and organize a weekend colloquium, where researchers could demonstrate their equipment and answer visitors' questions. In this way, each medium could add to the overall education experience by doing what it does best.

Science education is essential. But it is difficult, and it needs creative contributions from as many places as possible to succeed. No single medium can provide all the answers. However, with the cooperation of many different tools of communication, it is possible to enhance significantly the basic science education provided by the schools.

NOTES

1. Information about science centers can be obtained from the Association of Science and Technology Centers, 1016 Sixteenth Street, NW, Washington, DC 20036. Information about science museums and similar organizations can be found in *The Official Museum Directory*, published by the American Association of Museums, 1055 Thomas Jefferson Street, NW, Washington, DC 20007.

2. Quoted in "Philip Morrison—A Profile," *Physics Today* 35 (August 1982): 41.

3. Copies of the summary from this conference are available while supplies last from the Exploratorium, 3601 Lyon Street, San Francisco, CA 94123.

THE VIDEODISC/
COMPUTER MARRIAGE

Wally Longul

During the past five years, the emergence of the self-contained, relatively inexpensive microcomputer has shaken the educational establishment by opening up the opportunity for "distance education." Satellites and other communication carriers connect students and teachers who may be thousands of miles apart and provide learners with access to vast data banks. Computers attached to audiovisual equipment become teaching machines that can call up visual displays and point out areas of interest in them. With the increased use of personal computers and central information storage facilities, "formal" education may someday take a fraction of the time it now takes. Learning, on the other hand, may never end, as each computer provides daily, instant, up-to-date education in the home.

In a recent television special based on his book *The Third Wave*, Alvin Toffler said, "How literate is a child if he or she can't see through the distortions and propaganda on television or in other media? How literate is a child who knows nothing about computers? In fact, some people today are already speaking of tri-literacy: print literacy, media literacy, and computer literacy. We need to reinvent all of education—even the idea of literacy."

Mass media shape and manipulate people the way industrial machinery molds physical materials. With its wealth of diverse, everchanging information, broadcast television has shaped the way people—particularly young people—experience the world around them. Although frequently maligned, television has been a critically important education medium, bringing a sense of visual literacy to a public that obtains an increasing amount of its information through video screens. But broadcast television, always delivering its abundance of information in a predetermined order, provides a one-way learning experience that prevents the viewer from becoming truly involved. For years we have been passive users of television, our only point of interaction the on/off switch.

Then came "Sesame Street," and a generation of children who interacted with television in a new way learned to read and count before setting foot in

Wally Longul is an executive producer of science programming for TVOntario whose productions include "Fast Forward" and "The Third Wave."

a classroom. Now, new computer-based interactive learning technologies are starting to do away with the need for students to be in the classroom at all.

The telephone was our first universal, fully interactive telecommunications system. This system that we use so easily, with hardly a thought, has given us a common audio space with human beings throughout most of the world. Today, the computer has given us the capacity to make television interactive as well. Instead of passively viewing programming in a particular sequence, we can engage in a dialogue with the set. We can request data from anywhere in the world, about anything in the world, and it is available instantly, cheaply, and conveniently. New computer keyboards, better video displays, TV screens that are responsive to touch, computers that respond to voice and answer in synthesized speech: all of these technologies give us more control over information and more individualized learning choices than ever before. With infinite patience, the computer charts an educational path through complex subjects, presenting information at users' own levels of comprehension and delight.

The opportunities for all kinds of exploration and expression will accelerate with the increased use of the videodisc. Videodisc technology can provide a vast library of previously unavailable audiovisual material. In an article called "Experimenting with Videodisc," Rod Daynes writes, "With conventional instructional television, a program begins with the first frame and ends with the last. But on videodisc, with its capacity to random-access any one of roughly 54 thousand frames ([the equivalent of] 30 minutes of . . . passive program material), programs need not run continuously from the first frame to the last. Therefore, [the teacher] can design interactive strategies that allow the learner to become directly involved with the program."

Joined to a computer, a videodisc machine can show a television program backward, forward, in slow motion, speeded up, or in any order the viewer requests. Gone is the passive experience of broadcast television. The videodisc user can go straight to any part of the program by simply entering a location code into the computer. He can study each frame of the program separately, as though he were looking at a slide show, or move through any sequence of frames at his own pace. Or the computer can be preprogrammed by a teacher to move the videodisc material forward at a rate based on the learner's level of comprehension. The end result is a creative educational process that teaches students how to teach themselves.

Before the computer can teach a hundred different things, however, it must be taught a hundred different things. Once enough information has been stored in its memory, it can create total environments. It can simulate worlds that exist, that have been, that may be, or that never will be. Once a computer is programmed and married to a videodisc, young people can explore almost any place, from outer space to the small intestine!

Satellite dishes like these are beginning to make "distance education" a reality for Canadian children and their American counterparts. *Photo courtesy of TVOntario.*

Dr. Ludwig Braun of the State University of New York says that, with a computer, he can "provide students with discovery and learning experiences of a variety that was never possible before. I can develop simulations and games that permit students to get outside their ordinary experiences, that give them *Star Wars* or ... Tolkien ... experiences in biology or chemistry or physics or the social sciences."

Imagine for a moment what it would be like for a child to take a field trip into the far reaches of the universe. The visual images for the trip are stored on a videodisc and generated by the young "pilot's" choice of flight plan. The adventure is monitored by a computer that feeds back information on the pilot's choice of direction, thrust, and fuel consumption. Passing Venus or Mars, the pilot may want a closer look at the planet's surface (supplied by a still frame on the videodisc) or information relating to the surface temperature, planet size, or number and names of its moons (supplied by the computer). The pilot moves through space at his or her own speed, motivated by curiosity.

Or suppose a child's videodisc journey were through the human body. Exploring the workings of the digestive system, the child could follow a piece of fried chicken down the esophagus and into the stomach. Digestive juices flow into the stomach; the child wants to know where they have come from. He or she asks the computer, which answers by listing the organs that supply digestive enzymes. Which organ does the child want to learn about? The pancreas? Fine. A videodisc program on the pancreas begins. When the child tires of it, he or she presses a letter on the computer keyboard, and the remains of the chicken bite move on to the small intestine. The process of digestion can be interrupted as many times as the child chooses by questions and audiovisual explanations.

Other voyages are possible: through a giant redwood tree, from its roots to its leaves; into a pot of boiling water, to watch it turn to steam; or into the eye of a hurricane. The technology to accomplish these learning adventures exists. The problem is not hardware but software, and what is needed is not more educational software but different kinds, with programs that offer a more exploratory approach to learning.

In a recent interview on the TV program "Fast Forward," scientist and science fiction writer Isaac Asimov suggested that "no one should learn anything he doesn't want to learn. Once he learns that learning is a fun thing, he will want to learn other things as well. . . . If a person is interested in baseball, teach him baseball. He will want to learn to read to read about baseball. He will want to learn arithmetic so he can calculate batting averages. Once he learns that, he may discover that arithmetic is more fun than baseball. He just may."

There is an ancient Chinese blessing that says, "May you live in interesting times." We do! Computers and videodiscs in the classroom and at home are changing what is taught, and the way it is taught. In the future, computers will have the potential to provide interactive, virtually instantaneous access to unlimited information, transforming living and learning for people of all ages. "Distance education" will be everywhere, anytime we want it.

THE ECONOMICS
AND POLITICS OF
SCIENCE ON
TELEVISION

*The price of creative liberty is not only eternal vigilance but
also some continuing, guaranteed source of funding, for otherwise
talent and ability are diminished or lost.*

June Goodfield, *zoologist and writer*
Reflections on Science and the Media, 1981

It is one thing to discuss how television can supply more and better science
programming, and quite another thing to make it happen. Broadcasters are
obligated by law to operate in the public interest, but that doesn't mean that
they always—or even usually—serve the vast and varied needs of the American public. Commercial television broadcasters in this country do not tend to
take risks, and many of the largest cable operators appear to be falling into
similar "safe" programming patterns. Much of the responsibility for providing
a variety of TV programming not usually found on the commercial channels
has therefore fallen to public broadcasting. But public television programs are
supported by a combination of government, corporate, foundation, and viewer
dollars, none of which are easy to come by. If there is to be science on television, it must be paid for. By whom, and with what degree of government
involvement, are the questions that the essays in this chapter address.

In his essay, Les Brown, editor-in-chief of *CHANNELS of Communications* and author of a number of books about the television industry, takes a
realistic look at science programming's chances of surviving on broadcast and
cable television. Edward Aduss, the manager of corporate advertising for Gulf
Oil and a former science teacher, writes about Gulf's long-time support of the
"National Geographic Specials."

Congressman Albert Gore, Jr., from his dual perspective as a member of the House Telecommunications Subcommittee and chairman of the Committee on Science and Technology's Investigations and Oversight Subcommittee, looks at the dearth of science programming for young people within the larger context of commercial television's failure to serve young audiences with almost *any* kind of programming. Finally, George Tressel, a program director at the National Science Foundation who headed the NSF's Public Understanding of Science Program until it was abolished in 1982, examines in economic terms the success and failure of a number of different TV series about science.

HOW TV GOT HEALTHY—
IN SPITE OF ITSELF!

Les Brown

The bluntest truth about American television is that while its stations are licensed to serve the public interest, invariably they are operated to serve the owner's economic interest. Television is a business before it is anything else, and it is ruled by audience ratings because the ratings represent dollars.

One does not normally think of television as a teacher, but in fact it is marvelously suited to mass education. Anyone who doubts that has only to watch a football game. Every play is dissected and analyzed in careful detail and the important ones repeated on instant replay, and then repeated again in slow motion. People who watch football regularly on TV become well versed in the fine points of the game, even if they've never played it in high school or college.

But if commercial television declines to teach in more useful ways—if it does not point itself toward science, for example—it's because education does not serve the profit motive very well. Broadcasters are quick to argue that people don't go to television to learn something or be improved; they just want to be entertained. With football coverage, the teaching is part of the entertainment; audiences like seeing the plays repeated and having them explained. Education, in this instance, is simply good business.

Certainly, if broadcasters gave primacy to their public interest obligations, they would have concentrated from the earliest times on the dissemination of health information and the promotion of physical fitness. For what could be a more obvious service to the people than helping them stay alive? Instead, television operators shrank from this kind of education because, all too often, it conflicted with their advertising imperatives.

Do you advise people to walk everywhere they can when you're selling cars, tires, motorcycles, gasoline, and automotive parts?

Do you teach people to buy vegetables for health, when there are no fast-food chains pushing carrots, broccoli, and spinach?

Do you tell people that too much salt can be injurious to health, or too much sugar, when the junk foods advertised on TV are loaded with salt or sugar—and when salt itself is an advertiser?

Les Brown is editor-in-chief of CHANNELS *of Communications.*

Slim Goodbody educates children about their bodies and good health habits on "Slim Goodbody's Top 40 Health Hits," which can be seen on Nickelodeon, The First Channel for Kids. *Reprinted with permission.*

Do you urge people to go out and breathe fresh air when you want them home watching television commercials?

Television did not, until it was forced to, inform its viewers that smoking was a serious health hazard. Cigarette companies were spending some $220 million a year in television advertising when the Public Health Cigarette Smoking Act banished cigarette advertising from television in 1971. Broadcasters complained of discrimination: Why deny television and radio this important source of revenue and not newspapers and magazines? Because, the answer came, television and radio are licensed to serve the public interest, and the Surgeon General's report on cigarette smoking established conclusively that the promotion of smoking was not in the public interest.

I am at a loss to recall more than a few programs, leafing through the entire history of television, that were expressly oriented to health. Mainly what comes to mind are the old early-morning exercise programs, but they were more concerned with cosmetics than with fitness—the Body Beautiful rather than the Body Healthy. The heroes of TV's prime-time series were seldom ideal role models: they drank, smoked, fought, took chances, drove fast. A person who was conscious of his health was not glamorous, romantic, or heroic. Often he was ridiculed.

And yet, just when we thought we were turning into a nation of TV-watching zombies, poisoned by the tube, we have become instead extraordinarily physically active. More adults are jogging, walking, skiing, and playing tennis, squash, and racquetball than in any period of my lifetime. I'm not sure how to account for this, but I suspect that television—in spite of itself—has conveyed in its mindless way the vital health information. People are much smarter about their bodies today than they were ten or twenty years ago, and I attribute this to television fallout.

Because sports is a profitable form of programming, there is a lot of it on TV, and we have learned to lionize the athlete. Often we see these heroes in stretching or running exercises. We know that physical conditioning is partly what makes them good players. They talk about it in the pre- and postgame shows, as well as on the talk shows. Talk shows thrive on people who write books, and from time to time the books are on nutrition and fitness.

The stars of TV's prime-time entertainment series are usually well-built and have flat stomachs (William Conrad and Ed Asner are among the exceptions). Even though they may drink and drive fast, they send the message that fit is beautiful. Meanwhile, the revolution in television programming touched off by Norman Lear's "All In the Family" in 1971 opened the way for situation comedies and made-for-television movies dealing with such topics as manic depression, venereal disease, drug abuse, alcoholism, teenage pregnancies, and disabling conditions.

But perhaps even more important were the deaths of real-life celebrity-

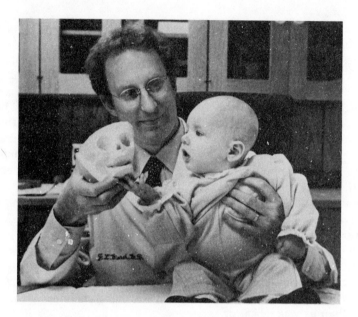

Four-month-old Lois Eaton and surgeon Dr. Jeffrey Marsh examine a precise plaster model of her skull: Lois's cranial surgery, which corrected the abnormal development of her head, was featured in one of the "Discover: The World of Science" TV specials. *Photo courtesy of "Discover: The World of Science."*

heroes, reported on the news, which alerted us to health matters: Edward R. Murrow, Natalie Wood, Elvis Presley, John Belushi, and many others.

Television news became profitable at around the time of the Lear revolution, and health specialists like Dr. Art Ulene and Frank Field were accorded regular segments in newscasts. In the eighties, there was an eruption of pop psychotherapists on TV—Tom Cottle and his ilk. The pendulum's swing to an interest in health matters on TV came from a perceived rise in the subject's popularity across the country rather than from the broadcaster's conscience. The more health information serves the business purposes of broadcasters, the more it appears on the tube.

Now comes cable, with its amazing channel capacity, and starry-eyed enthusiasts make predictions that there will be a channel for every interest— contract bridge, antiques collecting, science, horticulture, fashions. In fact, the same rules apply with cable as with commercial television, except that cable operators are not licensed to serve the public interest. Thousands of program services may be possible on cable, but only a few are feasible in harsh business terms.

Television—even cable television—is expensive to produce, and millions of dollars are at stake with nearly every national venture. Businesspeople do not readily take the plunge on long shots. At the start of 1983, there were forty-seven program services on the satellites aimed at the nation's cable systems. Most of them specialized in the types of programming that were already popular on commercial television: movies, sports, news, children's shows, and women's features. Two were related to science—Cable Health Network and The Weather Channel—both on the assumption that health and weather are popular topics.

The success of such specialized channels would surely have encouraged other entrepreneurs to invest in science-related services. But Cable Health Network and The Weather Channel had to compete for viewers' time with all the flashy entertainment on the commercial channels and the new pay-television networks. And so, early in 1984, Cable Health Network was forced to merge with another cable channel that failed to develop advertising revenues, Hearst/ABC's Daytime, a channel devoted to women's interests. The resulting new channel, Lifetime, focuses not only on health but on "life-style issues." The Weather Channel also failed to rally sufficient advertiser support but chose a different survival tactic: to impose a carriage fee to all affiliates carrying the channel.

It remains to be seen whether science will suffer a setback on cable as a result of these events. Other new media—videotext and the laser-driven videodisc, primarily—lend themselves admirably to continuing education in the sciences. They may enjoy a modicum of success in the new electronic environment, but neither is as yet a mass audience medium. We may find that for a long time to come the best hope for science on the home screen is on public television or in popular commercial television series that deal with science dramatically or by the way.

CORPORATE SPONSORSHIP: UNDERWRITING OUR TECHNOLOGICAL FUTURE

Edward L. Aduss

Should a corporation become actively involved in science programming on commercial or public television? The answer depends on a variety of factors, ranging from the quality of the TV program in question to the degree of management enthusiasm for the project. Certainly, Gulf Oil Corporation's experience with the National Geographic Society specials indicates that the benefits derived from such an involvement can be great.

In 1975, Gulf Oil Corporation agreed to become sole underwriter of the "National Geographic Specials," a widely acclaimed series of programs that frequently explore science and nature issues. The series had enjoyed limited success on commercial television for a number of years and, when Gulf entered the picture, was being shifted to public television.

There were those outside the Gulf organization who were skeptical about the series surviving for any length of time on PBS. That skepticism was unfounded, as subsequent events have proved. During the first eight seasons on PBS, the "National Geographic Specials" set new ratings records for public television, achieved critical acclaim, and received more than one hundred major awards. Late in 1982, Gulf agreed to continue its financial support for at least another three seasons to create a full decade of partnership with the National Geographic Society and Pittsburgh's public television station, WQED. By the end of the tenth season (1985), at which time forty individual specials will have been aired, Gulf's total underwriting commitment will exceed $36 million.

If there is a key to the success of the specials, it would have to be the fact that Gulf Oil chose to ignore the skeptics and to view the project as a unique opportunity and not a risk. Once committed to underwriting the series, the corporation decided it would protect and enhance its investment

Edward L. Aduss is the manager of corporate advertising for Gulf Oil Corporation and a former science teacher.

with advertising, promotion, and publicity. The validity of Gulf's commitment has been confirmed by the record-setting success of the first eight seasons of the "National Geographic Specials."

There are several reasons why a corporation might consider underwriting or sponsoring quality science or nature programming. One reason, obviously, is to be able to gain product and corporate exposure by running its commercial messages during the program. The corporations that advertise on commercial television understand this. There are, however, other more subtle reasons for sponsoring television programming. They relate to a responsibility to make possible programs that not only entertain, but also inform and educate.

It is often said that science and technology are truly reshaping our society and our lives as never before. People are concerned about these changes and are demanding to know more. The appearance of several new science magazines on the newsstand, regular science columns in the newspapers, and "popular science" shows like "That's Incredible!" on TV indicate that there is an increasing interest in "reality," a strong national market for science.[1] It is increasingly clear that if the public needs and wants to know more, our national institutions—and not just government—should help provide information.

There is, of course, a more selfish reason why corporations might be interested in supporting science programs. Since business depends on technology for its existence and profitability, it makes sense to do something that encourages young people to learn about science early in their lives so they will be more eager and able to apply it later in their careers. Educators tell us that if we are to develop the next generation of scientifically literate employees, these individuals must become interested in science at a relatively early age.[2]

Unfortunately, the nation's schools are in a constant struggle to maintain good science education programs because the subject matter is changing so rapidly. The problem is recognized by the Children's Television Workshop:

> Schools typically can provide only limited treatment of science at the elementary level and usually do not begin formal instruction in specific disciplines before the seventh grade—at about age twelve. But attitudes are quite often fixed by then. Science has become unappealing to many children, even before classroom instruction begins.[3]

To companies concerned primarily with the bottom line, these reasons may seem rather philosophical, even unimportant. But to ignore them is also to ignore the responsibility that companies have to the nation as a whole. In

"Gorilla" is one of the "National Geographic Specials," which are produced for public television with the support of Gulf Oil Corporation.
Photo by Anne B. K. Krumbhaar, © N.G.S. 1980.

some cases, the responsibility is already part of the corporate culture, as the
chairman of Mobil Oil Corporation, William Tavoulareas, wrote in an essay:

> Corporations reflect the values of society in which they operate,
> and American society today demands more of its corporations
> than provision of jobs and manufacture of good products.[4]

If the nation's schools are unable to provide adequate science education,
then the search has to go on for other institutions to do it. Television has the

potential to fill at least part of the void. It has long been recognized as an effective educational tool, not only as a way to show films on closed circuit in a classroom but as a way to shape "children's perception of reality."[5] The potential extends into the home, where, as psychologists Dorothy and Jerome Singer have said, television can "stimulate thought rather than produce a kind of mindless staring."[6]

From the corporate advertiser's point of view, a logical question is whether there truly is an audience for science and nature programming, an audience that would respond favorably to the company's support of such programs. The answer would seem to be that there is. And it is a growing audience. In the late 1970s and early 1980s, a number of new science shows were aired, including "Universe," "Cosmos," "NOVA," "Life on Earth," and the series of "National Geographic Specials." Some of these programs received high ratings, which made an impression on many corporate advertisers and TV producers.

It is not entirely accidental that many science programs have appeared on public television. It has been claimed that PBS has inherited a more academic approach from its roots in educational radio. But the PBS image has been changing rapidly. In the most recent five-year period surveyed, public television has more than doubled its share of viewers. In 1975, when Gulf Oil first underwrote a "National Geographic Special" on PBS, the average audience share was about 2 percent. In 1982 it reached 5.3 percent. Programs like "Cosmos," "NOVA," "Life on Earth," and the National Geographic series have clearly had an impact on that increase.

Is the future of science television therefore brighter on public television than on commercial television? That's a difficult question to answer. When a corporation like Gulf Oil has to choose between underwriting and commercial sponsorship, it must develop two separate sets of objectives, since there is little comparison between the two options. The approaches are different and so are the benefits.

The obvious difference is advertising: commercials, as we know them on commercial broadcasting, versus the lack of commercials, which we have become accustomed to on PBS. When buying time on commercial television, the advertiser has control over what his commercials will say and how the company projects its image or sells its product. Until very recently, on public television, the best that a corporate sponsor could expect was the mention of the company name and a logo on the screen for a few seconds; even the new experiment with commercials on PBS does not allow for product advertisement. Gulf was very aware of this difference when it elected to underwrite the "National Geographic Specials" and form a partnership with the National Geographic Society and public television. Even now, the reason for doing it may sound a bit "corny," as corporate management admits.

Mechanical engineer David Wilson and his recumbent bicycle are among the scientists and inventions featured on "The Search for Solutions," a series created for classroom use and funded by Phillips Petroleum. *Photo from "The Search for Solutions Teachers Guide," made possible by Phillips Petroleum.*

"I don't want to make us sound like a white knight or anything," says Thomas E. Latimer, senior director of advertising and corporate communications for Gulf Oil, "but we are the ninth largest corporation in America and we have a share of social responsibility. This is one way of handling that responsibility. We are trying to bring this quality television to as many Americans as possible. And it isn't just quality television, it is quality television that often highlights problems in the environment, another concern of ours." Gulf's chairman of the board and chief executive officer, James E. Lee, sums it up this way: "We see the 'National Geographic Specials' as a chance to help provide first quality, family-oriented television that is not just entertainment. These American-made documentaries, diverse in both subject and scene, are informative and advance public awareness. These are films of which we can be proud." In fact, there is a clear sense of corporate satisfaction and higher employee morale, even a sense of pride, in knowing that the company has a hand in the programs. As one employee said, "*Nobody* doesn't like the 'National Geographic Specials'."

There was never any doubt about the quality of the "National Geographic Specials," since the National Geographic Society coproduces the programs with WQED. But Gulf Oil saw the opportunity from another perspective—the perspective of generating an upscale and large audience for public television and the programs it chose to underwrite. This meant luring viewers away from prime-time, commercial network shows and getting them to turn on public television. To do that, Gulf developed and implemented a comprehensive advertising and promotional campaign designed to capture the imagination and interest of potential viewers. This kind of promotional commitment was new to public television. The campaign began by promoting the very first Gulf-sponsored special in 1975, "The Incredible Machine," which turned out to be the most watched program in public television history and which held that place until 1982. Recently, Gulf updated its advertising strategy by becoming the first major underwriter to buy time on commercial television to promote a PBS program.

What about the Gulf Oil Corporation's objectives? Are they being met? By almost every measure, they are. Today, ten of the "National Geographic Specials" are among the twenty highest rated shows on public television. During the 1981–82 season, the National Geographic programs had an average audience of 15.3 million viewers, well above the PBS average. "The Incredible Machine" headed the list of most-watched PBS programs until another National Geographic program, "The Sharks," surpassed it with a 17.4 percent audience share. This seems to bear out the claim that the viewing public will watch science programs if they are entertaining, well promoted, and of high quality.

It must be emphasized that, in the end, what has made the programs successful is not Gulf's commitment to promotion (although certainly this has been an important factor) but the shows' quality. The series began with high standards and has built on them. In addition to ratings achievements, it has received dozens of awards for both content and production quality. Included in the list of more than one hundred awards to date are six Emmys, and, significantly, citations from several science and wildlife organizations and a medical film festival committee. This is an obvious source of pride for underwriters.

Although acclaim was not a primary Gulf Oil objective when the corporation began underwriting the specials, acclaim has been one of the by-products enjoyed by all the partners that make these programs possible. But Gulf has received even more than acclaim. Every corporate underwriter hopes that its company image will be improved by association with the program the company supports, but that is by no means automatic. A research study conducted before the 1981–82 National Geographic TV season indicated that audience awareness of Gulf Oil as a series underwriter had attained its highest level since the research analysis began three years earlier. It is difficult to ascertain exactly what this public recognition means to a company, but in Gulf's case there is supporting evidence that it has helped the company's business. During each TV season, Gulf receives hundreds of letters from people who have seen the specials and want to thank Gulf for sponsoring them. Many of the correspondents also say they will buy Gulf products simply because of the company's association with the programs.

If a corporation is to properly underwrite quality science programs, however, a full financial commitment needs to be made. This will probably mean substantial money for advertising and promotion in order to build an audience, particularly if the program is to go on public television. Unless the viewers know the program is going to be on, they can't be expected to watch it. Luckily the awarding of grants or the agreement to underwrite a program on PBS is usually less expensive than purchasing equivalent commercial time on network television. This could be an important deciding factor if the budget for such activities is limited, as is often the case. Another important factor is the level of management support for public television sponsorship. At Gulf, top-level managers understand the objectives of the "National Geographic Specials" project and have been enthusiastic about the undertaking from the start.

In the final analysis, corporations choosing to sponsor or underwrite TV programming have to determine what their overall goals and objectives are and whether or not the proposed program or series logically fits their total corporate picture. For Gulf Oil, underwriting the "National Geographic Specials" makes sense in light of the company's energy development activities and resulting concern for the environment. Since the company was committed to underwriting a TV program anyway, one like the National Geographic series made good sense. Gulf's experience with the series proves that corporations and TV producers can combine forces to create entertaining and educational science-related programs. It is likely that the curiosity of the viewing public about science and technology has been stimulated through historical events like the space program, and through medical advances, high-tech industrial developments, and environmental concerns. It would seem to be the responsibility of those who stand to lose or gain by changes in technology to encourage the public's interest, to bring "reality" to the viewing audience.

Opportunities to do this on television are becoming more numerous. "The portrayal of science on television is still primitive, still in its infancy," says educator Jonathan Weiner. "Much more should be possible—even on programs meant for [only!] fifteen million people."[7]

But where does the responsibility really begin? Does it lie with the corporate manager who recognizes a social responsibility and has a desire to act? Or does it lie with TV producers who are willing to stray from the safe path and seek to develop the potential of television? As with so many questions, there is no single answer. Really effective partnerships between corporate sponsors and producers come about when both sides can develop not only a profitable financial arrangement but a common interest in quality programming as well.

NOTES

1. Jonathan Weiner, "Prime-Time Science," *The Sciences* (September 1980): 6–11.

2. Fred M. Hechinger, "About Education," *New York Times*, 15 January 1980, sec. 3, p. 4.

3. Joan Ganz Cooney, "Television and the Challenge of Science and Technology," Children's Television Workshop brochure on "3-2-1 Contact" (January 1980): 1–2.

4. William P. Tavoulareas, *The Bottom Line of Public Television*, one of a series of brochures in The Touche Ross Forum series (New York: Touche Ross and Company, 1981).

5. Susan Chira, "What Children See When Watching Television," *New York Times*, 6 January 1983, sec. C, p. 1.

6. Dorothy G. Singer and Jerome L. Singer, "Is Human Imagination Going Down the Tube?" *Chronicle of Higher Education*, 23 April 1979, 56.

7. Weiner, "Prime-Time Science," 11.

WHAT HAVE THEY DONE TO YOU, CAPTAIN KANGAROO?

Albert Gore, Jr.

At a Congressional hearing in March 1983, veteran CBS broadcaster Bob Keeshan gave us the terrible news. "Captain Kangaroo," as Keeshan is better known to millions of American children and grown-ups, was on the endangered species list. After appearing weekday mornings for twenty-six years, Keeshan's program for children had been relegated to weekends only and aired at an hour—6 A.M. in many places, 7 A.M. in others—when even children might not be watching. In addition, because the Captain's budget had been slashed, there were few new episodes in the works. Any child who got up at 6 A.M. saw mainly reruns. A year later, the show was cancelled.

"Captain Kangaroo" was the last daily children's program on commercial television. What happened to the Captain symbolizes the recent decline of children's television in general, and on the commercial networks in particular. To me, it underlines the extent to which opportunities are being missed in important areas of children's TV. One of these areas is science programming.

I must confess at the outset to a serious conflict of interest. As the father of four children under the age of nine, I am keenly aware of the role television plays, for better or worse, in young people's lives. We have all heard the statistics. Children from the ages of two to five watch television an average of twenty-seven hours a week, most of it adult programming. In families in which both parents work, television can have an even greater influence. In some homes, TV has become an electronic babysitter.

What I see happening now is a tragedy of great proportions. Children are our most important resource for the future. They need and deserve our careful attention to their personal development and education. But today, children's TV consists almost entirely of noisy, sometimes violent Saturday morning cartoon caricatures of real life. This surely is not enough. It may suffice for the sponsors of these shows, but it is not good enough for our children.

Albert Gore, Jr., (D–Tenn.) is a member of the U.S. House of Representatives. He serves on the Telecommunications Subcommittee of the House Committee on Energy and Commerce, and is also chairman of the House Committee on Science and Technology's Investigations and Oversight Subcommittee.

What can we who serve in Congress do about it? As you will see, attempting to solve this problem by legislation is awkward and problematic but may be the only avenue open.

It's not hard to understand what happened to "Captain Kangaroo." He was caught in the middle of one commercial network's race to compete with the others in a hot new contest for viewers of the early morning news shows. Those programs are profitable and promise what broadcasters call an "upscale" audience of well-educated adults who buy products. The children's audience isn't large and preschoolers don't buy cars or cologne. So, in his regular 8 A.M. time slot, "Captain Kangaroo" was an expensive liability. Eventually, he was rescheduled to make way for an expanded "CBS Morning News."

What can we do to encourage excellence in children's television in an atmosphere like this? In particular, how do we support essential programming that serves important needs like science and mathematics education when the networks are unwilling to support it?

Ironically, science shows for children, though few and far between, have been some of the most outstanding and critically acclaimed in the history of the medium. From Don Herbert's "Mr. Wizard" in my youth to the excellent PBS series, "3-2-1 Contact," by the Children's Television Workshop, TV science programs for youngsters best fulfill my own ideal for the kind of television I want my children to watch. These programs inform and intrigue young people, make them ask questions of their own, and absorb them in the mysteries of the Earth and our universe. They entertain, to be sure. But most important, they treat children as people, as inquiring individuals who are creative, imaginative, and capable of thinking and understanding.

Programs like "3-2-1 Contact" were formerly supported by the National Science Foundation (NSF) and its Public Understanding of Science Program. Funding from that program also helped establish shows like the PBS series "NOVA" and science coverage on National Public Radio. The Public Understanding of Science Program was eliminated in 1982's round of NSF budget cuts. But with the passage of the Emergency Mathematics and Science Education Act by the House of Representatives in 1983, many of us are now hopeful that new funding will soon be found for this valuable resource in science education.

The producers of "3-2-1 Contact" recently told Congress that they could turn out superior science programming for elementary school students for the next decade at a cost of $35 million. Like "3-2-1 Contact," these shows would be integrated directly into classroom and reading experiences. I think this is a laudable goal and I applaud CTW's efforts. I don't think, however, that the existence of PBS shows like "3-2-1 Contact" and of similar efforts on cable television should relieve commercial broadcasters of the responsibility they have under their licenses to serve the public interest. In a typical week, only

52.7 percent of all U.S. TV households tune in to PBS one or more times. Cable services, like Warner Amex's Nickelodeon, are watched by even fewer households and require a subscription fee for cable service. Commercial broadcasters have the financial resources, the creative talent, and the franchise that enables them to reach the entire viewing public, free of charge to the individual viewer.

The Federal Communications Commission is the executive branch agency responsible for issuing TV station licenses and for overseeing how well broadcasters carry out their responsibilities. But, in this Administration, concerned as it is with the deregulation of broadcasting, FCC oversight of children's television has been an extremely low priority. The FCC has turned from regulation by raised eyebrow to acquiescence with a wink and a nod.

The FCC issued a policy statement on children's television in 1974 which concluded that, as licensees of the public's airwaves, broadcasters have a "special obligation" to serve children as an "important and substantial" community group. At that time, the FCC ordered television stations to make a meaningful effort to increase the amount of programming for children and to air informational and informative programming for children. In 1979, five years after its mandate, the FCC discovered that programming for children had increased by less than one hour per week. Therefore, the FCC began a rulemaking proceeding to address the dearth of programming for children.

The present FCC chairman, Mark Fowler, has sent signals about his views on the future and proper place of children's TV. He has asserted that making broadcasters provide any programming for children at all amounts to a violation of a station owner's First Amendment rights. Fowler once suggested that if there is to be a place for children's TV, the function should be delegated to the Public Broadcasting Service. Oddly, his suggestion came at the same time the Reagan Administration was proposing cuts to the PBS budget for 1985–1986 totalling $110 million. Such cuts would almost insure that there would be no public television left to carry children's programming.

In this atmosphere, it is little wonder that commercial broadcasters have cut back in their commitment to children's TV which, economically at least, they consider an unattractive part of their programming mix. During the past several years, children's TV has begun to simply disappear.

Confronted with an avalanche of criticism from the public and from Congress, Chairman Fowler agreed in the spring of 1983 to reconvene the children's television rulemaking process shelved by the FCC in 1979; however, the results were less than encouraging for the future of children's programming. In December 1983, the FCC terminated this rulemaking proceeding and weakened its existing policy statement.

In effect, the FCC has recently decided that commercial broadcasters do not have to fulfill their responsibilities to provide programming services for a given segment of the viewing market. According to the FCC, if public broadcasting and cable television provide programming for children, commercial broadcasters can ignore their long-held obligations to nearly forty-four million Americans under the age of 12. As Commissioner Henry Rivera dissented at the time: "This is a funeral and my colleagues have here written the epitaph of the FCC involvement in children's television ... an abrogation of this agency's responsibility to unique and vulnerable beneficiaries of the FCC's public interest charter."

What options does the FCC or Congress ultimately have? One is to remove all regulations and policies on children's TV and rely entirely on broadcasters to police themselves. That clearly would be a disaster. To understand why, one only has to examine the marketplace dynamics that forced "Captain Kangaroo" off the schedule. In fact, the voluntary approach by broadcasters has left us with a situation where there is not one single regularly scheduled weekday program for children on network television. A second alternative would be to charge broadcasters a "spectrum fee" for the use of the airwaves. Income from such a fee could be applied to producing specialized programming, including children's television, and to paying the costs of airing it on commercial, public, or cable television stations.

A third alternative, one that is discussed a good deal these days, is to establish mandatory minimum programming standards for specific amounts and kinds of programming for children. A bill has been introduced in Congress which would require each television broadcaster to air one hour each weekday of educational programming designed for children. Given the current fervor to deregulate the broadcasting industry, this legislation may provide the last real hope to enact some countervailing proposals to insure that licensees adequately serve the special needs of children. At a minimum, it would remove the competitive disadvantages to any one station providing children's programming—the same market disadvantage that forced "Captain Kangaroo" into the Saturday morning children's ghetto slot.

I prefer still another alternative, one that has been repeatedly overlooked in the present rush to deregulation. It is an option that the FCC has never really tried, but which I consider the best and most equitable in the long run. We simply need to toughen the guidelines for public service programming and require stations to demonstrate their commitment to children's programming in order to keep their operating licenses. Under this option, the FCC would issue clear, explicit license renewal guidelines and actively police the stations. It would finally establish an enforcement policy that makes broadcasters at least a little uncertain about whether or not they will be able to keep their licenses without also providing good children's programming. I would link this approach to strong government support and encouragement of excellence in children's programming on public television and cable services.

Looking to the future, I believe other nonbroadcast television services will come to play an important and positive role in television for children later in this decade. Unemployed steelworkers, we read in the papers, are now using computer-aided instruction systems, like Control Data Corporation's PLATO, to teach themselves new job skills. Such programs for interactive instruction are already well established for children of all ages and produced by a number of manufacturers. Some of them, like the Massachusetts Institute of Technology LOGO teaching system, are available on plug-in computer game cartridges that use the home television for display. Such programs for creativity and personal discovery mean that children may soon become computer literate at the same time they learn to read and write.

On the horizon are even more powerful closed-circuit technologies that are hybrid combinations of television programs, computer instruction systems, and encyclopedic data banks. These new systems could be instrumental in exposing youngsters to science and mathematics at home at a very early age. And they hold out the potential for allowing parents to take control of the television again and begin to alter its impact on our children. If television must be the babysitter in some homes, one alternative for parents is to seek out better forms of the medium—an electronic babysitter that can teach and stimulate growth rather than simply mesmerize with flickering colored images.

As for broadcast television, particularly at the network level, I believe we will continue to fight an uphill battle. We all know we need better children's TV. But it will take concerted, continuing pressure from many sources—the FCC, Congress, educators, parents, and organizations like ACT—to bring about change. Ratings, demographics, and all the other economic measures of success in the television industry fail badly when it comes to assessing and satisfying our children's needs. Broadcasters need to be reminded—prodded, if necessary—to look up from their bottom lines and to examine what television at its very best could be offering children. If they fail to do that, broadcasters will be missing a critical opportunity for our society. And they will have convinced at least one observer that they are unwilling and unable to carry out their public trust.

As Captain Kangaroo, Bob Keeshan, said recently before the House Telecommunications Subcommittee: "I am a broadcaster, a producer of programming. I am not unfettered; I am responsible for my actions and for the effects of my programming on our young people. I accept that responsibility and ask that I be held accountable. I ask that each and every one of my fellow broadcasters accept that same accountability."

SUPPORTING SCIENCE: A STAND AGAINST LOWEST-COMMON-DENOMINATOR TV

George W. Tressel

One gains insight into the kind of "science" programming that can result from the commercial networks' quest for the highest possible ratings by taking a look at a current series which enjoys reasonable success. Several years ago, the production company responsible for the program solicited material for its new series with the following letter:

Dear Journalists and Independent Producers:

... I just want to clarify the basic format and scope of "Incredible Sunday," and give you a precise idea of what we are looking for.

First of all, the title has been changed to "That's Incredible!" .... [T]he Executive Producer of the series has been responsible for the "In Search Of" series ... many of the National Geographic Specials, and "The Undersea World of Jacques Cousteau."

The show is one-hour magazine format. ... The specific categories:

- ESP (training, experiments, new uses)
- Medical (new medical achievements, research, experiments, new findings)
- Animals (used in scientific experiments; any being used by the government; dolphin research, unusual chimps, etc.)
- Science (astonishing scientific achievements; frog research, etc.)
- Unexplained (UFO stories; paranormal phenomenon; world's greatest natural mysteries; archaeological findings, etc.; voodoo, witchcraft)
- Human Interest (amusing stories, cults, zombies, etc.)

George W. Tressel is a program director in the office of science education of the National Science Foundation. He was director of the NSF's Public Understanding of Science Program until it was abolished in 1982.

"Walter Cronkite's Universe" was aired by CBS for three summer seasons between 1980 and 1982. *Photo reprinted with permission.*

- Stunts (not magic, not tricks—amazing, daring feats; incredible stunts)
- Haunted Houses (anything we can substantiate)
- Future (wacky things like robots that we might be using in the future)
- Skeptic (things on the market claiming one thing that we're skeptical about)

We're looking for . . . cults, curses, stories about premonitions, anything along the lines of Tutankhamen, archaeological findings. Paranormal phenomenon is very big. A few stories in the works here: a psychic who finds oil and precious minerals; zombies in Haiti; voodoo nurses in America; a computer that predicts weather twenty-four hours in advance; biofeedback research for stress; freshwater amoeba that eats brain cells.

... Stories should be of redeeming educational interest; should be zany and topical; should amuse, enlighten, amaze an all-family audience.

Such letters and the programs that grow out of them represent commercial broadcasters' attempts to find the common denominators of interest among the nation's TV watchers, which in some cases becomes the *lowest* common denominator. It is not surprising that broadcasters are relentless in this quest. We are constantly promised that broadcasting can and will become a glowing tool of mass culture and enlightenment. But, stepping back from discussions of what television *should* be and *could* be and *might* be, we are left with what television actually *is*: an agent of trivial diversion. Whether they are children or adults, most of the more or less one hundred million people watching television each evening are tired, bored, and seeking a transient and entertaining distraction. After all, only small groups attend uplifting lectures and debates, while audiences of millions go to rock concerts and football games. Television is not likely to change these preferences.

Public broadcasting is dedicated to more altruistic goals and tries to serve the needs of smaller audiences, many of whose members are seeking informal education. But PBS faces many of the same realities as commercial broadcasting and suffers from a painful ambivalence. The $250 thousand per hour investment in a typical PBS production is economical only when divided among audiences of millions, and whenever the audience is less than awesome, the system is subject to charges of elitism. So public television, too, searches for the common interest. But not too avidly, of course, lest it threaten commercial interests or appear a carbon copy of commercial television.

With a few exceptions, then, mass communication implies service to a mass interest. This need not necessarily be service to its lowest common denominator, but the resulting audience must be of sufficient numbers to warrant the per capita cost and allocation of limited air time. Children, for example, represent a substantial audience segment whose indirect purchasing power is highly focused and significant, if clustered in a non-adult viewing time such as Saturday morning, but insufficient to compete for attention at times when the far larger adult population is available. Thus, almost all non-Saturday children's programs are found only on public television, and, in fact, most children, most of the time, watch adult television.

Like the child audience, people interested in science are a minority audience within the enormous TV-viewing public. According to a 1980 opinion survey conducted by Jon D. Miller, Kenneth Prewitt, and Robert Pearson, twenty percent of the public is actively interested in science and another twenty percent is curious.[1] This is enough interest to spawn a number of suc-

The Disney Channel, a cable television service for young people, offers a science program called "The Scheme of Things," which is hosted by Mark Shaw. *Copyright ©* *Walt Disney Productions 1983.*

cessful science magazines, a science section in the Book-of-the-Month Club, and an increasing focus on science in newspapers and general interest magazines. But it is not enough to create a role for science in the only medium that reaches the entire nation.

This was not so in the past. In the early days of television, "Mr. Wizard," which ran on NBC from 1951 to 1965, was a household word. Countless numbers of today's scientists and engineers recall sitting with batteries, bells, and wire to wait for their friend to come on the air. "Mr. Wizard" was born at a time when programs were largely spawned, funded, and produced by advertising agencies and independent producers, well before the dominance of networks and the discovery of the lowest-common-denominator profit machine. The program happened to suit the needs of the Cereal Institute, which was seeking a showcase for its "eat a good breakfast" message. Today this kind of "institutional" advertising would not be attractive to cereal manufacturers, and the program, with its comparatively narrow audience and quiet pace, would not be attractive to commercial broadcasters.

In a somewhat similar manner, pioneer television producer Don Meier created "Wild Kingdom," which, after two decades on the air, is one of the longest-running commercial television series. Here, too, the program was developed independently and sold directly to the sponsor, Mutual of Omaha, which in turn negotiated its incorporation into the NBC schedule. The wildlife series went on the air in 1963 and proved very popular. It was securely established as a lead into the NBC prime-time schedule until the FCC established the "prime-time access" policy in 1971 and mandated that the early evening time period be allocated to locally scheduled materials. At this point, Mutual of Omaha chose to syndicate the series, marketing it station by station. Surprisingly, the result was a significantly increased overall audience. The proprietary interest of local stations resulted in a substantially greater promotion effort, and the series faced comparatively weaker competition from local programming on other stations.

During the 1982–83 season, "Wild Kingdom" aired on roughly three hundred stations. It remains a vigorous contender outside the network system, having found a way to serve the smaller "family" audience with a relatively low-budget program. It is interesting to speculate whether such a series could have survived as part of an increasingly competitive network schedule. It may well be that the rules restricting network dominance have provided an important haven for programs such as "Wild Kingdom" with their more specialized appeal.

The greatest TV science success story is PBS's "NOVA." Until recently, the series was funded by a combination of support from the National Science Foundation, the PBS Station Program Cooperative, and industrial underwriters. Although it only covered about ten percent of the total cost, the NSF support provided a stable base and a prestige that helped producers secure funds from corporations like Exxon, TRW, and Johnson & Johnson. The audience for "NOVA" is loyal and growing; estimates of over ten million viewers are not uncommon, indicating that there is a substantial "special-interest" audience for thoughtful and penetrating discussion of science. Perhaps this evidence, together with the growing market for science magazines, helped to encourage CBS to experiment with a science series.

In 1980, at the urging of Walter Cronkite, CBS undertook to test a "magazine" format science program, "Walter Cronkite's Universe," as a summer series. For producer Jon Ward, there was never any question but that the program had to reach a commercial-television-sized audience; the limited viewing public of "NOVA" simply would not do. From its beginning, the program posed a challenge: find material and present it in a style that would attract and hold the attention of at least thirty percent of all the people looking at television on a given evening (in other words, an audience share of thirty). The task was formidable. After all, the public opinion study by Jon Miller and his colleagues found that only twenty percent of the nation was actively interested in science. When, at the end of the 1982 summer season, "Universe" had fallen to an audience share of less than twenty, the series was canceled.

Some people blamed the show's shrinking ratings that last summer on its poor placement in the week's schedule and on CBS's failure to promote it adequately. In addition, it was preempted three times in fifteen weeks, which is certainly not conducive to the development of a loyal audience. Still, the fact remains that the series failed. Perhaps there is a "formula" for creating and promoting a science program that will attract a large, general audience, but CBS did not find it.

Luckily, however, we *have* found ways to bring some science programming to a smaller TV audience. With an astute investment of about $3 million per year, and cooperative funding from other government agencies and industries, the National Science Foundation has established a number of successful science series on both public and commercial stations. Like "NOVA," most of these reached audiences of between five million and twenty-five million—not large by commercial broadcasting standards but very impressive in most other arenas. Two examples of these NSF-supported successes are the West Coast TV series "Synthesis" and National Public Radio's science reports. Then there is "Star Date," which has aired on more than one thousand radio stations and has become a viable commercial entity, and also "3-2-1 Contact," the daily children's science series. "How About," a series of weekly science news spots by Don Herbert (Mr. Wizard) is now incorporated in the local news broadcasts of over a hundred commercial TV stations. The audiences for all these programs represent a large and still unsatisfied public interest in science. They challenge producers to supplement the efforts of our formal educational system with TV programs that inform and stimulate interest among children while helping parents to become more aware of the importance of science and technology.

Broadcasters, weary of interest groups forever demanding changes in the medium without seeming to consider the economic realities behind the commercial television system may wonder, "Is science so important?" In this highly technological world, the answer is, "Yes!" We cannot remain leaders in technological fields—including telecommunications—without a continuing supply of scientists to generate new ideas, engineers to convert these into new products, technologists to operate and maintain the systems, managers and investors to weigh new investments, teachers to train new scientific experts, sophisticated legislators and regulators, and a scientifically knowledgeable public.

Our current concern about scientific training in the U.S. is raising questions about the way our education system is organized. A number of other nations have centralized education systems, and today many of these countries' governments are placing top priority on the need for technical education. (In Russia, for example, where math and science are a national priority, some two million high school students are now studying calculus, a subject studied by only 150 thousand American high school students.) By contrast, in the U.S. we believe that schooling should offer choices. Most students in this country are not told what they must study; they follow their interests and often postpone career decisions until quite late. Many switch areas of study and develop a versatility that lets them enter or participate in fields that were not foreseen when their education began. Thus, the U.S. education system is one of immense flexibility. But it is greatly dependent upon communication, popular understanding of our society, and awareness of new developments and potential careers. To function, it requires a public that understands the thrusts of science and technology. The long-term success of our open-ended approach to education depends upon citizens who are informed enough to make enlightened choices.

It is naive to relegate this responsibility for informing the public about science entirely to the schools. Parents and children learn about science and technology from other sources, largely television, newspapers, and magazines. We cannot afford to communicate an image of scientists and technologists as long-haired, wild-eyed Frankensteins any more than we can afford to believe that all businessmen are manipulative and unethical. Yet large numbers of our children have come to believe that science is difficult and dangerous, and that the discipline of mathematical and technical studies is too exacting for all but a peculiar elite. As a result, many children, with their parents' implicit consent, decide that mathematics and science are not very important, and they choose to avoid learning the basic skills of tomorrow's society. Some would argue that television, with its emphasis on the importance of pleasure and instant gratification, is a major cause of children's decision to avoid something they perceive as "too hard.",

There are those who say that new video technologies will change all this. We are promised that they will revolutionize the scale of mass communication, bringing to it a range comparable to that of the publishing business. Videodiscs, videotapes, pay-television, and a variety of related electronic magic tricks will take the place of today's monolithic networks, opening an FM-radio-like range of inexpensive delivery techniques that will give us a world of endless video options, a world where parent and child can share the joys of educational programming whenever they like.

Somehow, the authors of these promises see the potential but pass over the problems of who will produce and pay for this enormous supply of costly, special-interest material. Somehow, they seem unconcerned by the persistent evidence that the public seems far more interested in paying for commercial-free movies and pornography than for education. No one has yet found the key to a viable "quality" cable channel, although many millions of dollars have been lost in the search. I hope that one of the current telecommunications experiments will come up with an economic basis for such programming; perhaps a system of variable-rate, pay-per-program television can be devised. But I am not very optimistic.

The promoters of cable and other new technologies are right about one thing: if television is really going to be a significant adjunct to popular education, it must serve a smaller audience than the common denominator. Someone must set aside the valuable air time and absorb the cost of producing and showing special-interest materials on a very expensive medium. Perhaps this cost can be covered by a marketplace system; but if so, we have not discovered how. In spite of the success of "NOVA," "3-2-1 Contact," and "How About," there is no indication that shows like these could continue without external support. We can provide this support through government subsidy or through corporate altruism—or through a combination of both. We might, for example, consider ways to "tax" the broadcast system, either directly or through regulatory maneuvers like the prime-time access policies. But, in any case, *someone* must pay for materials that are both costly and vitally important to a viable society. Who is it going to be? Our children and grandchildren are waiting for the answer.

NOTE

1. Jon D. Miller, "Scientific Literacy: A Conceptual and Empirical Review," *Daedalus* 112 (Spring 1983): 29–48.

THE PROOF OF THE
PUDDING

Attempting to educate the public in science is difficult. . . .
The stakes, however, are very high, and we have no choice but to
try—and, as we try, to endeavor to learn how to try even harder
and better—and to remain undaunted by defeat. . . . What is the
alternative? To leave the world to the National Enquirer, *the as-*
trologists, and the creationists? . . . Never!

Isaac Asimov, biochemist and writer
"Informing the Public: Why Bother—The Case For"
SIPIscope, January/February 1982

This chapter looks at some examples of science television programming: public broadcasting's "NOVA," which has been on the air since 1974; "Synthesis," a series of public television documentaries shown between 1977 and 1982; "3-2-1 Contact," the Children's Television Workshop series, which has had two seasons and will soon go into production on a third; "The Body Works," a syndicated children's program about human anatomy produced in 1979 by commercial station WCVB-TV in Boston; "Simply Scientific," a series of animated films for classroom use produced and distributed by Learning Corporation of America; and "The Voyage of the *Mimi*," a dramatic series produced as part of a new science curriculum package for Bank Street College of Education. With the exception of the last essay, all of the essays in this chapter are written by producers who are, or were, closely involved with the programs they are describing.

"NOVA": HOW IT BEGAN

Michael Ambrosino

"**N**OVA" was a challenge and a model.
We felt challenged to create a series that would tell powerful and exciting stories about the workings of the world, stories that would entertain and
stimulate viewers to discover more about the topics and issues they raised.
We also wanted to create a model for public television. We hoped that these
new documentary programs, thoroughly researched and delightful to watch,
would help launch new series from American-based production centers that
would deal with other "serious" subjects in the arts, sciences, and humanities.

Developing "NOVA" took three years from idea to first broadcast, and
it all started with a letter I wrote in 1971 from a rented flat in London. I had
left my job as associate director of programs at WGBH-TV in Boston, and the
family and I were enjoying the last days of my year-long attachment to the
BBC as the Corporation for Public Broadcasting's "American Fellow Abroad."
I'd spent the fall working on "24 Hours," BBC-I's exciting and often controversial daily news and current affairs program. My wife Lillian, one of the
founders of Action for Children's Television, was conducting research on children's programs in Europe, and our children were attending school.

I'd spent the last few months studying the BBC's Features Group. There,
hundreds of producers made programs that involved topics usually considered
academic: science, technology, art, music. The subjects were often complicated, but the productions themselves were not. The results were understandable, enlightening, and quite enjoyable.

My letter, then, carried a rather simple proposal. We should develop
such a production group at WGBH and begin by creating one project, an
American counterpart to BBC's science series "Horizon." I proposed a new TV
series, a continuous run of broadcasts that would combine some American-
made films with some coproduced with the BBC "Horizon" staff and others
purchased from around the world. This cooperative arrangement would keep
costs low, promote high-quality productions, provide a greater quantity of
films for the same price, and help us all get started. The percentage of American films would be low to begin with, about thirty percent, and grow grad-
ually to fifty percent. Unlike "Masterpiece Theatre," which purchased good

Michael Ambrosino is president of Public Broadcasting Associates, Inc., and was the
creator and first executive producer of "NOVA" and "Odyssey."

"Life (Patent Pending)," a "NOVA" program about genetic engineering, examines new developments in biotechnology and their consequences. *Photo by Mike Lutch.* © *1982 WGBH Educational Foundation.*

plays, this new series would use the BBC's creative talent to develop new American production capacity. Our films were to use a "process approach," often reaching back in time to fashion the historical trail of past discoveries, examining in detail the physical and mental processes of scientists. They were to be active films, involving locations and laboratories all over the world, seeking out stories that involved the relationship of science to society and U.S. public policy.

Looking back more than ten years, "NOVA" seems to have happened very quickly. But it is hard to forget that first year spent working out the details of programming, staffing, and budgeting, and a second difficult year devoted to fund-raising. (That year, 1972, President Nixon vetoed the public television bill twice.) Without the support we received from Carnegie Corporation of New York, the Corporation for Public Broadcasting, the National Science Foundation, and Polaroid, our science series would still only be a dream.

Late in the spring of 1973, we were ready to hire staff: three BBC producers from London and a group of young American researchers and assistants. We opened up a wing of WGBH's new film production center and started our research for the first series of programs. I settled on the title "NOVA": "a bright new shining star." It seemed appropriate, and few would understand the double meaning: novas fade and die, just as do many bright new ventures in public television.

But it worked! The first twelve programs were broadcast in the spring of 1974 and were followed rather breathlessly that fall by seventeen more. Each season since, "NOVA" has returned to PBS, and now its archive of wonderful films provides a year-long library for public television stations in America.

The aims set down in my 1971 "NOVA" proposal seem to have aged well in these last twelve years.

1. Make "NOVA" for the public; too often science films are made only for scientists.

2. Choose stories about specific tasks or problems that illuminate larger issues, not the other way around.

3. Demonstrate the creation of new data and concepts.

4. Show science as a human enterprise.

5. Involve the viewer in the process of experimentation and discovery.

6. Explore alternatives, effects, and consequences, especially when dealing with technology.

7. Attempt to move the viewer to action—perhaps just to seeing the world from another point of view.

"NOVA" has developed and grown. Four successive executive producers have molded and shaped it in ways to match their vision. Many of its staff members over the years have moved on to other series and their contributions to public television have been significant. "NOVA" has also worked as a model. "Frontline" and "Odyssey" are two direct offspring, and many other series have gathered strength from the fact that "NOVA" continues to draw large and involved audiences.

When "NOVA" was announced to the assembled members of the American Association for the Advancement of Science in 1972, I ended with these words, still appropriate today:

I envision a television which is more than a stream of pleasant experiences, but one which may also be a river of unsettling adventures prodding the viewers to explore, to look into themselves and become alive to the entertainment of their own minds.

"NOVA": THE MAKING OF TEENAGE SCIENTISTS

Linda Harrar

> *Four years ago I started filling balloons with hydrogen. I wanted to see how much force they had when they exploded. So I took a candle, fastened it to the end of a stick, and I lit the balloon. There was such an explosion that it knocked me right down off my feet. From then on I decided that hydrogen would be quite a powerful fuel to use.*
>
> Tim Tylaska

Not many scientific careers have had such literal launches. Tim Tylaska, of Mystic, Connecticut, has been trying to design himself into motion since he was about three years old. His backyard is littered with the remains of past science projects. First he built a man-powered flying machine—a bicycle with his mother's drapes for wings. Then it was a go-cart fueled by mothballs, followed by a hang glider made out of Hefty trash bags.

I met Tim while producing "Adventures of Teenage Scientists" for the "NOVA" series on PBS. He was one of forty high school finalists in the 1982 Science Talent Search, run since 1942 by Science Service and funded by Westinghouse Electric Corporation. The Talent Search has become so successful at identifying future scientists that it has earned the nickname the "Nobel Farm Club." Five Nobel Laureates are former Westinghouse winners.

Approaching this TV program, I had a double mission in mind: first, to find out how young people get involved in science; and second, to point out that problems with science education are turning away all but the most motivated and persistent students. Interviewing the Westinghouse winners was a little like interviewing the Rockefellers for a program on the unemployed; I hoped that by showing what works for some, we might learn what isn't working for the rest.

Possible titles for the program came quickly to mind: "The Whiz Kids of Westinghouse" or "Einsteins in Blue Jeans." But after spending two months with these teenagers, I learned that the stereotypical whiz kid or genius label

Linda Harrar is a producer for "NOVA" at WGBH-TV in Boston.

didn't fit. The Westinghouse winners may be science superstars, but they don't seem all that different from their peers. Several are only average students. But somehow they discovered, early in life, the joys of intellectual challenges, and now they are hooked on the high entertainment that goes on in their brains when they wrestle with an idea. Many winners have had strong support from parents, teachers, or brothers and sisters. Someone along the way helped them get turned on to science. This is one of the things separating them from other bright kids in their classes.

To compete in the Science Talent Search, one thousand high school seniors write a major research paper on a topic in science or mathematics. Westinghouse hosts all forty finalists for a five-day stay in Washington, D.C., where they exhibit their research at the National Academy of Sciences. Ten students are selected to receive major scholarships, but all forty are considered winners.

For his project, Tim Tylaska built a hydrogen engine. It runs on tiny, foil-covered fuel pellets which, when dropped into water, release hydrogen gas. When we met, Tim held out his hand and quietly introduced himself to me, looking just past my left ear. I moved closer, trying to hear better what he had to say. It must be very important to him, I thought, if it was worth getting past all this shyness to say it. He told me tales of homemade parachutes, catapults, Tesla coils, wind tunnels, model rockets, tennis ball cannons, hydroplanes, and diving bells.

Although he has become more careful about safety in recent years, a strong theme of danger and risk runs through Tim's projects. I asked him if he didn't worry about blowing himself up. He said, "Stuff that is really different is usually dangerous. If it weren't dangerous, then everybody would do it. I get a feeling that I have done something that no one else has done, maybe because other people have been afraid to, not because it couldn't be done."

Willingness to take risks was a quality that I found in most of the Westinghouse winners: social risks, in that they have learned the value of communicating with new people; and intellectual risks, in that they're not afraid to take up new ideas. In fact, that's how they get their kicks. More playful pursuits, such as hanging out in the parking lot, they find boring. At an early age they develop a keen sense of pleasure in hard work and intense scientific activity.

A longtime judge for the Talent Search, Dr. David Axelrod, says, "I continue my involvement in the Search because I enjoy the excitement of a burning young intellect. Also, I find that each year's group is a good barometer for what's happening in society. For instance, during the Vietnam War the kids were long-haired and disheveled. They were also very aggressive and grilled us with questions about bombing Cambodia and the role of science in the military. I doubt if this year's group knows we *have* a foreign policy."

Tim Tylaska tries out one of his flying machines on the "NOVA" episode "Adventures of Teenage Scientists." *Photo by Peter Argentine.* © *1982 WGBH Educational Foundation.*

I, too, found the latest crop of winners noticeably uninvolved in politics. They seemed to have little sense of what science can do to society, and what a powerful force it can be. Perhaps that awareness will come later, with maturity. Right now, they are concentrating on being extremely busy high school students, with an array of nonscientific interests that range from modern dance to music. They have learned early how to concentrate well and organize their time, and they like competing in a variety of fields.

Gary Griner of Huntsville, Alabama, is an average student who loves any sort of competition. In his junior year, he won Alabama's state pole vault championship. He shares his interests in sports, music, and science with his father, an aeronautical engineer. "I was between science projects and ran across a picture of a seismograph in a book," explains Gary. "I thought to myself, 'What do I know about seismology?' That was a great place to start. I had nowhere to go but up!" It was Gary senior who brought home the plans for the seismograph his son built. Gary junior says, "If it weren't for my father, I don't know if I ever would have finished the Westinghouse paper before the deadline. He was right there with me at 2 A.M. in the final days."

Marathon runner Jonathan Taylor was president of his senior class in Bayside, New York. He plays the violin and viola in his spare time—whenever that is. Says Jonathan, "I feel I don't miss out on anything. I do the things I do because I enjoy them. I view myself possibly as a fledgling scientist, but right now I think I'm just a plain, ordinary high school student."

Jonathan's elder sister Naomi is a former Westinghouse winner who did research with leeches. It was she who procured the silkworms for Jonathan's project on the "Bactericidal Effects of Chlorhexidine Diacetate and Organotin on Silkworms Infected with *Serratia marcescens*." Jonathan recalls, "I discovered a long time ago that my sister was very possessive. She took over the entire kitchen to do her biological research. I was always interested in what she was doing and sometimes helped her. She even wanted me to feed the leeches by letting them suck the blood out of me.... But there are limits to what a brother will do for a sister."

Making a terrible mess in the house is the first condition for becoming a scientist, according to former Westinghouse winner and Nobel Laureate Dr. Sheldon Glashow. Glashow also remembers being a member of the Protozoology Squad at New York City's Bronx High School of Science: "There were a lot of us who commuted to the school on the subways. I would say to my friend Steve Weinberg [with whom Glashow later shared the Nobel Prize], 'Quantum mechanics is easy. I learned it last night.' And he would be very worried. So he would come back the next day and say, 'You may know quantum mechanics, but I know the calculus of variations.'"

Not everyone who wins the Westinghouse is going to go on to win a Nobel Prize. And not all of the Westinghouse winners attend specialized schools like the Bronx and Stuyvesant High Schools of Science in New York. But they do all come from families that place a high value on learning. And for the most part, they come from schools that provide a good education in science.

There doesn't seem to be any great mystery about what makes good science education; good teaching and an environment where children are challenged to learn are more important than fancy equipment. Ted Seiler runs a very special industrial arts class at Stuyvesant in which each student makes his or her own telescope. He fashions workstands for the class out of old cafeteria tables mounted on lead pipes anchored in potato salad buckets filled with concrete. Seiler says proudly, "Stuyvesant is not a new school; it's a good seventy-five years of age. But we have a good faculty and a group of students that are hungry for knowledge." Seiler sends his kids down to Canal Street to get the grit needed for grinding the surface of the telescope mirrors. Westinghouse winner Richard Chang enjoys the two-month task of grinding the mirror by hand: "It can be monotonous, but for me it's very relaxing. It provides a healthy balance for all the academic courses I am taking."

Thirteen members of the 1982 group of finalists were women, including Reena Gordon, the top scholarship winner from Midwood High School in Brooklyn. Reena is the daughter of two teachers. She combined her ability in math with her love of English to create a mathematical linguistic model of how the brain processes ambiguous sentences.

The number of women among the Westinghouse finalists is slowly increasing. But it is still an unhappy fact that women become discouraged at an early age from continuing in mathematics and science. Reena saw this happen to a number of her female friends and nearly gave up on math herself after one year with a poor teacher. Fortunately, the following year she had a better teacher who inspired her to stay with it. In making the "NOVA" program about the Westinghouse competition, I hoped Reena's success would encourage younger girls trying to decide whether or not to stick with science.

Jené Spears of Detroit's Renaissance High School was the only black student among the group of 1982 Westinghouse winners. She attributes her success in science to her own hard work and to encouragement from her parents. They took her to a model solar home, which sparked her interest in phase-change research. Jené also had inspiration from a very special teacher, Frank Pavia. Starting with the ninth grade, Pavia makes science projects a requirement for all his students. He even mounts them right onto the classroom walls—all the way up to the ceiling. "That way, even if my students are daydreaming," he points out, "what will they see? Science projects!"

Pavia explains, "Today we read a lot of material, look at a lot of TV, and everything is there pat. . . . If we want to know something, we go to the library. But who looked this up in the first place? How do we learn in the first place? We learn by doing operations on the outside world."

This hands-on approach to learning is echoed among all of the Westinghouse winners. To get engaged by science, students have to try doing it. They have to know there's a problem to be solved, dive in, and get their hands dirty. Even from the best of minds, science demands long hours and hard work. Science is constantly changing; it is not a dry set of static facts that one reads in a textbook. You have to run fast to keep up with it.

"NOVA" has stayed a strong series in part because its diversity reflects the kaleidoscopic nature of science. Many things that help broaden the appeal of "NOVA" to a wider audience also increase its appeal to young viewers: good stories, exciting cinematography, clear writing, and attention throughout the hour to humor, music, and occasional sound surprises. We know that "NOVA" has younger viewers, but we don't know how many. Most of our information comes in anecdotally from people who tell us their kids loved

"Animal Imposters" or "Whale Watch." Certain subjects, such as X-ray astronomy, will probably always lose the younger audience, as well as some adults.

I don't think "NOVA" should consciously set out to attract a young audience, but we should take care that we are continuing to make at least some programs that people of *all* ages will want to watch. I suspected from the start that "Adventures of Teenage Scientists" would draw a younger-than-usual audience. I hope that it has shown young viewers the fun and excitement that science can offer and has encouraged them—the average students as well as the superstars—to try their hand at it.

"SYNTHESIS": THE CONTROVERSY OVER CREATIONIST SCIENCE

Jeffrey W. Kirsch

There are certain events and issues that capture the attention of the public and awaken it to a problem that many did not know existed. The launching of Sputnik I by the Russians was such an event. By placing a small package of technical instruments in near-earth orbit, the Russians showed they were not afraid to challenge Americans to a technological race into space. Our national reaction, once the initial shock had passed, was a demand for the government to develop our scientific capability and to mobilize our youth for study and employment in what we now call the aerospace industry.

Today, one could make an analogous case for the commercial success of Japanese high technology products. Although it has been a sequence of developments over decades, and not a single, climactic event, that has led to Japan's penetration of U.S. markets, one might expect that the government and electorate of the United States would once again respond forcefully to the challenge from beyond our borders. But this time, the national response is tempered by a decade of uncertainty and disillusionment with scientific and technological progress. Americans are just now becoming aware that our system of science education is producing a small, well-educated elite to direct our nation's science establishment, leaving the vast majority of the population with only the rudiments of scientific literacy.

I was a producer of science-oriented public television programs from 1974 to 1982. It was only during the last year of my tenure that I was jarred into perceiving this reality of the American educational system while overseeing the production of an hour-long documentary on the creation-versus-evolution controversy that has emerged in schools across the nation. How ironic that while scientists are designing genes and probing the innermost forces of atomic nuclei, there are Christian fundamentalists who are seeking

Jeffrey W. Kirsch, Ph.D., *is executive director of the Reuben H. Fleet Space Theater and Science Center in San Diego, and was director of the KPBS-TV (San Diego) Science Center for six years. He was project director and executive producer of KPBS's "Synthesis," a public television documentary series.*

to revamp biology, physics, and geology curricula in the image of the Biblical creation story.

As executive producer of the five-year-old "Synthesis" project, a public television effort which produced twelve documentaries on science-related issues, I came to recognize Americans' combination of pride in achievement and anxiety over threatened values as a reflection of their ever-present ambivalence over the role of science in our society. As I look back on the development of the "Synthesis" project, I can see that we changed our approach to reporting on policy issues involving science and technology to reflect our awareness of Americans' mixed feelings about science. Nowhere is this more evident than when we turn our attention to issues affecting children, such as the conflict over the theory of evolution. Although our productions were not targeted to young children, I believe the lessons we learned about science, education, and the pluralistic nature of American values are relevant to the questions raised in this volume of essays.

The "Synthesis" project was established with a grant from the National Science Foundation. The grant money was to be used to produce documentaries on high-visibility policy issues in the western United States that were strongly associated with "progress" in science and technology. Our goal was to integrate the scientific and technical aspects of a controversy with a report on its sociopolitical impact. The producers were aided by a panel of seven scholars, reporters, and policy analysts who assigned priorities to topics, provided leads and contacts to the producers, and gave advice on the accuracy and balance of our programs.[1]

In our first sequence of programs, "Synthesis" I, we stayed very close to our original objective, producing policy reports on the Alaska oil pipeline, California water projects, and short-term screening tests that detect potential carcinogens in the environment. A fourth program was an interview with Dr. Frank Press, the director of the Office of Science and Technological Policy under President Carter.

"Synthesis" II continued the policy report format established earlier, but we introduced a new facet to our programs so as to broaden our viewership: the interaction between science and values. This new approach was most evident in the productions "The Grand Canyon: Who Needs It?" and "Closing the Learning Gap." With the former, we sent our cameras to the bottom of the Grand Canyon with a team of scientists and Colorado River motorboaters to get a better understanding of the ecology of the area and the wilderness experience. Our intent was to show that different beliefs about what constitutes a wilderness experience (and its value to the human condition) were at the core of a controversy over the U.S. Department of the Interior's decision to ban motorized riverboat excursions down the Colorado River.

"Creation vs. Evolution: Battle in the Classroom" was a special in the "Synthesis" series that examined the conflict over creation science. *Photo by Dotti Corser, courtesy of KPBS-TV, Public Television in San Diego.*

"Closing the Learning Gap" was the first "Synthesis" program to deal with an issue directly influencing children. We sought to determine why elementary school administrators have been slow to adapt direct instructional curricula for use with disadvantaged youngsters. These special curricula involve scripted lesson plans, rewards for good performance, and student responses in unison to teachers' questions. In some cases, these educational techniques had been effective in raising students' test scores. Yet school principals were concerned that the increase in the educational efficiency of these "scientifically" developed teaching methods was not worth the risk of stifling students' creativity and discouraging them from reading for pleasure.

During the production process we found ourselves grappling with the problem of showing how such value judgments by school administrators and teachers impeded the rapid introduction of sophisticated techniques that depended on conditioning and what appeared to be rote learning. To give our

TV audience the experience of direct instruction lessons, we filmed inside the classroom. In a particularly powerful scene, the teacher dropped pieces of pre-sweetened cereal into the mouths of students when they performed well. Through these and other classroom scenes, it became clear that behavioral modification techniques were built into the direct instruction pedagogy.

Our program contained comments by teachers, educational psychologists, curriculum experts, and a few parents. In our zeal to cover this controversial debate in the educational community, however, we failed to include the reactions of the students themselves. On reflection, I rationalized their exclusion: there was precious little time in a thirty-minute program, and what do kids know about the issue anyway? But somehow these reasons didn't satisfy my uneasiness, and I began to consider the possibility that we had missed a vital dimension in our story. Of course students are not experts in educational or cognitive psychology, but they can give their impressions and speak to the heart of the matter more directly than others. Their reactions, presented in a balanced manner, would be important for a viewer of any age to hear.

In "Synthesis" III we decided to focus our attention on topics that would further explore the relationship between science and values. Part of this new emphasis came from the realization that some of the earlier "Synthesis" policy reports had failed to explore the core elements of a controversy because the reports had become bogged down in details. We also hoped that by focusing on the pervasive influence of science and technology on the way people live, think, and feel, we could expand our viewing audience from its one percent and two percent ratings. Our new approach was epitomized by the "Synthesis" III program "Creation vs. Evolution: Battle in the Classroom," which dealt with the challenge to the educational system launched by the so-called creationist movement. The latter generally consists of Christian fundamentalists organized into local pressure groups which seek to establish the Biblical creation story in biology curricula as an explanation for the development of life on earth. Creationists claim that creationism is as valid as evolution and that enough scientific evidence can be assembled to justify teaching the creation story as science rather than as religion.

During the fifteen months we worked on the program, we found that the creationist controversy is symptomatic of a general malaise in science education that could reach crisis proportions if no action is taken. The problem posed by the creationists transcends the question of whether evolution or creation is "good science" because many people, adults and children alike, do not know what "good science" is.

Based on our experiences with "Closing the Learning Gap," we knew we should make an effort to understand both the parents' and the children's attitudes toward the issue. So, in addition to taking our cameras into the classroom of a public junior high school and a Christian day school in order to show their different approaches to teaching natural history, we also sought the personal reactions of the families involved. This proved to be difficult, since many creationist parents refused to be filmed or to give permission for their children to be interviewed on camera. However, by going into the schoolyard to sample children's opinions, the producer was able to determine that many of the youngsters were disappointed with a local school board decision to ban the teaching of the creation model as science in the public schools. As one of them remarked about his teacher, "He didn't push creation or evolution. He taught them both equally." And another fifth grader asked us, "Why should they teach one side and not teach the other one?"

Of course, there were also a number of students who were aghast at the conflicts between science and religion that were part of this particular teacher's lessons. They, too, were represented in the program. But the offhand comments of the students in the schoolyard had a tremendous impact on me. The students' appeals for fair play and equal time for "creation science" represented the value systems of many families. Their simple, direct statements were an exclamation point in the program, demonstrating how easily children could adapt to a "two model" approach to natural history if that were what their schools chose to teach.

Thus, the kids' remarks underline the great responsibility of teachers, school administrators, and school boards in choosing curricula. Elementary school children are *not* able to tell real science from pseudoscience. Nor, for that matter, are many adults able to make such a distinction. To the children who want to give creation equal time, the Biblical story is just another set of answers. They do not see that the creationists' "answers," which do not stem from scientific questions and scientific methods of investigation, cannot be science. This confusion illustrates a major problem in science education. Too many of us have been taught to expect answers from science, not questions (just as many people have been taught to expect only answers from their religion). But science is not a one-way street to the truth. Science is a process by which theories, replicable experiments, and observations are used to construct conceptual models that describe events and phenomena. At the heart of this process is the obligation to question the range of validity of any model. That is what scientists do when they "do" science! Unfortunately, it is not what we usually teach in schools, nor what we choose to relate to the public via the media.

In our "Synthesis" III production "Creation vs. Evolution: Battle in the Classroom," we tried to present a balanced, journalistic account of the technical and social features of the creation-versus-evolution debate, punctuated by sequences that demonstrated the arguments for both sides. Our goal was not to convince "true believers" on either side that they were right or wrong.

Rather, we wanted to reach the vast majority of people who had not yet confronted the controversy. In doing so, we wanted to make them aware that, while in this instance it was science curricula under attack, the tactics employed by creationists could just as easily be used by other groups to question teachings in other areas, such as history or English, and to offer "alternative" interpretations of these subjects.

The program attracted a relatively large audience for a public television documentary. It was carried by practically every public television station in the U.S. and was seen in three million households across the country. Over half a million people viewed "Creation vs. Evolution" during two prime-time broadcasts to the New York audience alone; the program attracted a five percent share of the television households both times it was aired. There has also been a large audience response to the program, primarily from people who liked it but were shocked to learn that there is still a controversy regarding evolution in our schools. And there was criticism, both from those who felt we were unfair to the creationist position and those who felt we were wrong to give the creationists "equal time." Our response to the latter concern has been that in a journalistic account of a debate, both sides must be represented fairly.

All of these responses have indicated that the program did what it was supposed to do: make people think about science in its relation to their values and to society as a whole. Most encouraging have been the letters and requests for transcripts from teachers and religious educators. From their interest in obtaining videocassettes of the program for use in classrooms, we believe the program will eventually reach many more students than those who saw the national broadcast in their homes. For example, a San Jose, California, high school science department chairman wrote:

> Congratulations for an outstanding production.... Could I have your permission to use my videotape copy in my biology classes? I am currently developing an extensive unit dealing with pseudosciences. This is partly to give a clearer understanding of science, by contrast, and partly to establish the clearly pseudoscience nature of "Scientific Creationism" before we study evolution. This approach would show why we can't include creation "theory" as a scientific alternative to evolution.

Another note came from a music teacher in Louisiana: "It was an excellent presentation, and I plan to use your program as a basis of discussion in my church school classes."

I suspect we will be hearing from teachers, students, and school administrators for many years to come. My hope is that the program will help them to think about the nature of science. The lesson I have learned from our coverage of this issue is that we need to change the way we teach science. The confusion between what is and is not scientific arises because we have too often been taught science as if it were a body of knowledge that provides answers. Rather, it should be taught as a method of inquiry that makes it possible to ask better questions about the way we perceive nature. This understanding of science as a process is what children's television can and should strive to impart to young viewers.

NOTE

1. Among these advisors were: David Perlman, science editor of the *San Francisco Chronicle*; Dr. Clifford Grobstein, professor of biology at University of California, San Diego; Dr. Gerald Cormick, director of the Office of Environmental Mediation at University of Washington; Dr. William Waters, professor of forestry and entomology at University of California, Berkeley; and Dr. Joel Primack, professor of physics at University of California, Santa Cruz.

"3-2-1 CONTACT": MAKING CONTACT

Kathy Stroh Mendoza

In our technology-dependent society, basic public policy decisions require an understanding of how science works, how technology is applied, and the trade-offs and options presented by each new technological development. Questions involving energy, resources, defense, pollution, and land use confront every major industrial nation. While statesmen and scientists study the challenges created by our new technologies, most of the public—particularly children—enjoy and use them without thinking or evaluating their impact. They disco on plastic roller skates, prepare frozen dinners in microwave ovens, watch the launch of the space shuttle on TV, play interactive video games, or listen to music on cassette players. As they grow up, these children will need to become more familiar with the science and technology that is affecting their lives and their environment. As mature citizens, they will need to develop a sound basis for making judgments about how to conduct scientific research and how to utilize emerging technologies. As jobholders, many will need to develop skills in science- and technology-related fields. To respond to these needs, society must see that children's introduction to science comes at an early age.

As a major step toward bringing children into contact with science and technology, the Children's Television Workshop produced "3-2-1 Contact," a television series on science and technology targeted to eight- to twelve-year-olds. The series of sixty-five half-hour shows was funded by a unique partnership of public and private funds, involving the National Science Foundation, U. S. Department of Education, Corporation for Public Broadcasting, United Technologies Corporation, and CTW itself. "3-2-1 Contact" premiered on more than 270 stations in the Public Broadcasting Service in January 1980, and the first season of sixty-five shows has been rebroadcast many times. A second season of forty shows, funded by the National Science Foundation, U.S. Department of Education, and Corporation for Public Broadcasting, was released in the fall of 1983.

The Children's Television Workshop is a nonprofit educational institu-

Kathy Stroh Mendoza is a White House Fellow whose assignment is special assistant to the Secretary of Defense. She is the former executive producer of "3-2-1 Contact" and coproducer of the "The Search for Solutions" series.

The young cohosts of "3-2-1 Contact," season I, interview engineer and space suit designer Vicky Johnson. *Copyright © Children's Television Workshop 1979.*

tion dedicated to experiments in mass communications. Since 1968, CTW has produced over two thousand hours of goal-oriented TV programs, including "Sesame Street," the educational series for preschoolers, and "The Electric Company," which teaches basic reading skills. With "3-2-1 Contact," the challenge was to use the entertainment and informational techniques of broadcast television to spark children's curiosity about science, to show them the scientific world that surrounds them, and to portray science as worthy of their interest and involvement.

From its inception, "3-2-1 Contact" was designed for at-home and in-school viewing. The TV show is intended to support and supplement existing science teaching. While the series does not attempt to present a comprehensive science curriculum, it does provide real science content and information, produced in an entertaining way to arouse the student's interest. The programs deliberately raise more questions than they answer, so that students are encouraged to explore on their own.

In American schools, a systematic science curriculum does not usually begin before the seventh grade. CTW's researchers found that children have already formed attitudes toward science and scientists before they begin science courses. While most children acknowledged the value of scientists to society—particularly for inventions and for curing illnesses—many perceived science as an unattractive field by and large. One study revealed that by the end of elementary school, twenty-five percent of the boys and only three percent of the girls said they would consider careers in science and engineering. A National Science Foundation study noted that women occupied only eleven percent of science and engineering jobs, while minorities held less than three percent of those jobs. With the hope that the broadcast could positively influence children's attitudes toward science, a panel of academic experts, researchers, producers, and writers devoted more than two years to studying the series' feasibility. They established broad series goals:

- to help children—especially girls and minority youngsters—recognize science and technology as a cooperative human endeavor open to their participation.

- to help them become familiar with styles of scientific thinking so that, as they grow, they can analyze important social issues related to science and technology;

- to help children—especially girls and minority youngsters—recognize science and technology as a cooperative human endeavor open to their participation.

Our title, "3-2-1 Contact," gave focus to our work. The challenge was to bring many different people with different talents together in partnership to produce a series of sixty-five half-hour shows in a very short time. The differences in our backgrounds made the task complex. Our group included researchers who had conducted extensive formative research for two years; they knew the audience but lacked the technical know-how to make the shows. There were content specialists who could tell us what scientific information was important and accurate; they knew their disciplines but were not always sure how to share what they knew with children. Add to this mix producers, who knew how to make films but were not always comfortable with science, and actors, who had to learn to interact with scientists. During the early stages of production, it became clear that before we could communicate with our audience, we had first to learn to communicate with each other. In order for our collaboration to yield the best results, we had to build a team capitalizing upon the strengths of many different specialists. We proceeded according to a management model CTW called "the collegial process."

Scientist Raymond Olzowy explains that these orchids are identical because they are clones on "3-2-1 Contact," season II. *Copyright © Children's Television Workshop 1983.*

Clear operational steps organized our production and defined the jobs some 350 people would undertake.

Structure: Weekly Theme and Daily Concept

The head writer and the content staff divided the series into thirteen weeks of daily programs. Each Friday's program, intended especially for in-school use, summarized and reviewed that week's learning. Each week was organized around a theme—a set of opposite concepts, such as Hot/Cold and Fast/Slow. The staff defined each theme in an essay, presenting a broad spectrum of interdisciplinary material organized under daily headlines. To draw out the most important scientific ideas for each daily show, they wrote explanations for the headlines. From this "bible" proceeded all work on the series.

Story Research

One of the major strengths of television is its ability to transport viewers all over the world, turning them into explorers. Our television program took children mountain climbing in Wyoming, scuba diving in Florida, and volcano watching in Hawaii. It was the story researchers' job to collect program material for locations such as these from personal experiences, newspaper and magazine clippings, lectures, and other sources. Stock footage researchers found out what material already existed on film.

Format and Production Techniques

A "magazine" format was adopted, allowing many different production techniques within a single show, including documentary material, drama, animation, graphics, stock footage, and studio taping. Many of the story ideas were best understood by using more than one production technique. For instance, to explain how a hot-air balloon works, a documentary showed one of the series' hosts riding in one. This segment was followed by animation demonstrating how molecules of hot air move to make the balloon rise.

Schedule

To keep us all on time and within budget, the executive producer and production manager laid out a master plan that set schedules which ended with each program's air date. Material that would take the longest to complete was commissioned earliest. There were some drawbacks to this approach. It meant animation, with a lead time of three months, had to be commissioned first, although it would have been preferable to commission the animation *after* we knew which concepts filmed in documentary form or in the studio required further illumination.

Preparation

Representatives from Research and Content, the head writer, and the executive producer briefed each field producer for each segment of the show. The content staff prepared the briefing sheets, giving producers background and suggesting possible questions. The researchers, our proxy for the audience, would study the notes and ask, "Will the kids understand what is being shown and said? Are we talking down to the audience? Is the film idea logical and easy to follow?" After the field producers had been prepared, they, in turn, briefed the crews and the cast. By long distance and in person, the content people screened and briefed the scores of working scientists and engineers who were filmed for the series.

By our selection of program hosts and guests, we intended to communicate to children that young people and adults are engaged in exciting and rewarding scientific pursuits. The three young hosts, only a few years older than our audience, were shown throughout the series as competent and involved. The actors who portrayed them were encouraged to ask questions of their own, which required them to think and participate fully in the production. They became very used to working this way and have since reported that this is one aspect of their CTW work they miss now that they have returned to their bread-and-butter world of commercials.

Studio

Studio wraparounds were taped last, to take into account the length of individual segments and to provide continuity and transitions from one segment to another. The studio allowed us a controlled situation in which to tape hands-on experiments for kids to do at home. The content staff suggested most of these experiments and supervised taping to insure accuracy.

Screenings

Our series contained over one hundred documentaries, and scores of animated sequences, stock footage pieces, and commissioned films. Each of these segments was screened in rough-cut and in fine-cut by the research, content, production, and writing staffs. Research would check for understanding and vocabulary. Content would check for accuracy. Production concerned itself with whether the piece would make good television. Writers judged how the segment would fit into the completed half-hour script.

This screening process was difficult, time-consuming, and sometimes trying, but it improved the shows and eliminated inaccuracies. We hired a full-time coordinator to make sure everyone had transcripts, everyone arrived at screenings on time, and everyone handed in critiques. No film, no show assembly, no release print went forward without approval from everyone. Differences were settled by Production after taking into consideration each of the voices in the collegial process.

The making of the first season of "3-2-1 Contact" was as rewarding as it was complex. By the time we were done, we had all learned a lot. Researchers knew much more about production. Content experts learned how to take the time to explain what they knew to nonexperts. Production teams were less hesitant to tackle a film on science or technology. And the actors had developed considerable experience as interviewers. Had we not encouraged everyone to participate fully in the process, our shortcuts would have been apparent to ourselves and, more importantly, to our television-wise young audience.

CTW started with the idea of making a science show for children. Before we could teach others, we ourselves had to understand how science works and how technology is applied. We could spark children's curiosity about science because ours had been sparked. We could show children the scientific world that surrounds them because we had marveled at it. We could hope to make science worthy of children's interest and involvement because we had come to regard it as worthy ourselves.

Have we made contact? Letters from our audience tell us we have. One girl asked why rain fell in drops instead of in a steady stream like the water from her faucet. Another asked what a platypus is because she was studying them in class. One described her class outing to the woods, where "we saw all the things you show on TV." Children were participating by doing: trying things out at home, in school, and in clubs. Many offered ideas that were incorporated in the second season of the series. These are the first steps in developing a nation of involved citizens, able to deal with the complex issues they will confront as responsible adults, and better able to shape the future.

"THE BODY WORKS": SCIENCE DOESN'T HAVE TO MEAN PBS

William C. Brennan

In the late winter of 1978 I was producing Dr. Tim Johnson's program, "House Call," at WCVB-TV, the ABC affiliate in Boston. The show's format involved an interview with a guest specialist, followed by viewer phone calls. "House Call" had been successful for several years, so station management decided it was time to expand into wider areas of health programming. Perhaps because of my background in children's programming at NBC, I decided to try an experiment. I invited a group of preadolescents into the studio for a special question-and-answer version of "House Call." Dr. Johnson used an anatomical model, various charts, and props to answer the kids' spontaneous questions. He turned out to have a talent for explaining complex topics in an understandable and entertaining way without sacrificing scientific accuracy. What was just as important, however, was the kids' reaction; they loved it!

Based on this experiment, Bruce Marson (then program manager), Steve Schlow (then executive producer), Tim Johnson, and I met to plan a series of five programs for young people with Johnson as host. Our theme was to be the human body—its major systems (respiratory, circulatory, digestive, etc.) and some of its "best" parts (eyes, ears, brain, etc.). What we came up with was part "Mr. Wizard" and part "Let's Take a Trip"—a combination of questions and answers, in-studio experiments, and on-location visits. We wanted to be able to discuss a particular question about science or medicine inside the studio and then, instantly, take our viewers outside to make a comparison or create an analogy.

In our first program, for example, we compared the efficiency of a local chemical factory to that of the human liver. We hoped to make science and medicine more accessible by using locations and activities from everyday life as illustrations. Also, to increase the accessibility of the scientific content, we wanted our series to have young "regulars" with whom our audience could identify. As our young cohosts' questions became more and more a part of

William C. Brennan is an executive producer at WCVB-TV in Boston who was responsible, with Dr. Timothy Johnson, for "The Body Works."

the show, it was our hope that the audience would be encouraged to ask questions and guess the answers along with the cohosts, even compete with them at home.

We knew how important it was to make "The Body Works" entertaining. A TV show that recreates a teacher/student relationship between host and viewer connotes, to most young people, homework, performance pressure, and enforced limits. Few young viewers will watch an entire program that too closely reminds them of a school atmosphere. But throw out the rules, make it entertainment, and you might keep them.

The first five "Body Works" episodes aired in Boston at 8:30 P.M. as half-hour specials shown between August 1979 and April 1980. The next eight programs were alternated with repeats of the first five to create a thirteen-part series that ran between September 1980 and June 1982. The programs' ratings were competitive due partly to the fact that adults watched with their children. Dr. Johnson had strong local appeal and national recognition through his syndicated series, "Update on Health," and his weekly appearances on "Good Morning America." This added adult audience helped make the program more attractive to advertisers usually not given to support of children's programming, and Dr. Johnson's reputation and name were easily promoted. So we were able to begin syndicating the series in the fall of 1979. Eventually it reached seventy percent of the nation's TV households.

Recognition and promotability were key to the whole distribution process. While everyone is quick to point out the merits of educational programming about science and medicine, there are few examples of its *commercial* success. "The Body Works" with Dr. John Smith would not have been syndicated and might not have been more than a one-shot deal in Boston. The success of "The Body Works" indicates that a local broadcast, well promoted and tied into local hospitals, research, and technology, can be a commercial success. On the other hand, the same program is probably going to be at best a "hard sell" for national syndication unless it involves a nationally known host or familiar actors.

"The Body Works" received many letters from viewers, primarily young people and teachers. The youngsters wanted to appear on the program, and the teachers wanted transcripts and broadcast times so they could tape the shows. Due to the number of requests from school systems, "Body Works" was made available on cassette for school and home use. One school system in Oregon based an entire week of science classes on five consecutive days of "Body Works" programs aired as after-school "specials." Other teachers used the cassettes in the classroom and followed up with quizzes.

If asked what I would have done differently in producing "Body Works," I'd say that I would have spent more preproduction time planning and organizing the medical and scientific material. It is not easy to organize

Dr. Tim Johnson demonstrates how our joints work on "The Body Works." *Photo courtesy of Metromedia Producers Corporation, Boston.*

material on a subject as vast as the body's circulatory system into three approximately six-minute segments! We had to repeat this "shrinking" process for all our programs, and with the advantage of hindsight, I can see inconsistencies in focus and overall presentation. In addition, it would have benefited the program to have been thought of from the beginning as a thirteen-part series. Instead, the first five shows were done with the idea of running them as Dr. Timothy Johnson "specials" for young people. After the first five shows proved successful, it was decided that we would produce five more. Shortly after production began on show number four of the second five, the decision was made to complete a package of thirteen shows. Up-front planning for the final total would have resulted in a more coherent presentation.

In light of the recent evaluations of public school education in this country—especially in math and the sciences—and given the many hours our younger population spends watching television, it behooves all of us in the communications industry to strive to create programs that make science an entertaining and functional part of young people's lives. Nevertheless, I believe that programs focusing only on specific areas of medical or scientific endeavor unrelated to everyday life will be unlikely to draw large audiences of young viewers. Instead, commercial broadcast television might try a relatively unexplored form of science programming for young people that ties together current events and science information. Topics such as airborne pollution, space technology, waste disposal, robotics, lasers, and holography are frequently in the nation's news. Programs for young viewers could incorporate current events into discussions and demonstrations of various scientific processes.

One stumbling block in the path of this approach might be a reluctance on the part of commercial advertisers to have their names associated with any potentially controversial issues. Yet a program using an event of international or national significance to explore scientific principles, if it were done well, might attract enough attention—and a large enough audience—to benefit the sponsors in the long run.

"SIMPLY SCIENTIFIC": FILMS FOR THE SCIENCE CLASSROOM

Robert McDonald

In 1979, Learning Corporation of America realized that educators had a very real and specific need for elementary-level science films. As one second-grade teacher plaintively told us, "There are so few good aids to convey basic science concepts to young children; we need all the help we can get!" So the idea of the "Simply Scientific" series was born.

Even before the first film in the series was made, we had certain criteria in mind. Above all, we wanted to produce the kind of high quality, entertaining films for which LCA is known. It also seemed clear that our new science series should consist of animated films with simple story lines, because our educational consultants advised us that such a format would best convey information at the primary school level. They also suggested that, for pedagogical reasons, each film should cover only one area of inquiry. Would we try to base the films on children's books, or would we commission original scripts? That, we decided, would be determined by the availability of suitable books in the areas we wanted to explore. If no appropriate book existed, we would create our own script with the help of advisors.

Enter *The Ordeal of Byron B. Blackbear.* This children's book, discovered in the normal course of story development, had all the elements we were seeking. It even provided us with a series title. "Why, that's simply scientific," quips one of the characters. "Simply Scientific" has since grown to a series of five films.

1. **Byron B. Blackbear and the Scientific Method**
   Dr. Alfred Clothears formulates "Operation Sleeping Bear" to discover an answer to a question that's been vexing him: How do bears know when to hibernate? He researches the topic using the scientific method, identifying each step as he proceeds. The film emphasizes that science is both process and knowledge; it encourages kids to regard science as an

Robert McDonald is vice president of production at Learning Corporation of America. His credits include "Simply Scientific."

"Simply Scientific" gives children a fun lesson about the composition of the earth in "How to Dig a Hole to the Other Side of the World." *Photo courtesy of Learning Corporation of America.*

endless quest rather than a finite body of information. (Based on *The Ordeal of Byron B. Blackbear* by Nancy Winslow Parker; Dodd, Mead & Co.)

2. **Beyond the Stars: A Space Story**
   A small boy looks out his bedroom window at the stars and asks, "Do people live on them?" In answer to his question, this film is a factual overview of the solar system, galaxy, and universe. It's also a colorful, fanciful outer space journey that introduces the planets and the concepts of gravity and weightlessness, and Fahrenheit and Celsius temperatures. (Based on *A Space Story* by Karla Kuskin; Harper & Row.)

3. **How to Dig a Hole to the Other Side of the World**
   This adventure in geology takes kids on an amazing educational journey through the layers of the earth to the very center—and back to the surface again. As the film's young explorer makes his way from topsoil to molten core, each geological term is fully explained. His fantasy trip is a memorable introduction to the wonders of earth science. (Based on the book of the same title by Faith McNulty; Harper & Row.)

4. **The Lightning and Thunder Case**[1]
   Set in the Wild West and told in a courtroom scenario, this tale sets the
   record straight about the most misunderstood and feared "bandits" ever
   to roam the land: the dreaded Lightning and Thunder gang. When the
   film ends, viewers are left with accurate scientific information, safety
   rules, and the reassuring feeling that lightning and thunder are positive
   phenomena that deserve respect. (From an original script.)

5. **Microcomputers: An Introduction**
   Young Jennifer introduces cousin Jeff to the fundamentals of microcomputers, and the duo manages to apply what they've learned to catch a
   crook. The film covers the many uses of microcomputers, explains how
   they work, defines the terms involved in their operation, and emphasizes the importance of human intelligence and judgment in programming and operating computers. (From an original script. Advisor: Dr.
   Mary Humphrey, Educational Microcomputer Consultant, Palo Alto,
   California.)

The series has been enthusiastically accepted, I'm glad to say. Preview
committees in schools and libraries (LCA's cornerstone markets) automatically
request new films in the series as they are released; a very high percentage of
these previews are retained for purchase. The films are then used in the classroom to supplement the standard science curriculum. (Each film is accompanied by a leader's guide written by a teacher, which contains a film summary, vocabulary words, questions, and suggestions for class and individual
projects.) Schools and public libraries have used the films for special programs
on science and safety, and as educational entertainment for story hours.
We've also had orders for "Simply Scientific" from teacher training programs
in colleges. And it's worth noting that reviewers in key educational journals—
including *Science Books and Films*, the toughest critic of films of this sort—
have given the series good marks.

Instructional television is probably the medium that's made "Simply Scientific" accessible to the greatest number of viewers. ITV (also called ETV, for
Educational Television) refers to the broadcast of materials over public television stations primarily for classroom use. The daytime slates of WGBH in
Boston or KQED in San Francisco, for instance, are made up of ITV programming (indeed, both stations have aired "Simply Scientific"). Decisions about
which programs to broadcast are generally made by local stations during preview sessions arranged by the four ETV networks: SECA (Southern Educational Communications Association, Columbia, South Carolina); CEN (Central
Educational Network, Chicago); PMN (Pacific Mountain Network, Denver);
and EEN (Eastern Educational Network, Boston).

"Simply Scientific" received excellent evaluations from ETV networks when it was first offered in 1981. The series has since been aired in forty-one states, making it available to many school districts that otherwise might not be able to afford it. (ETV materials are leased, not sold, with the fee based on a formula that includes the length and number of films in the series and the number of students in the viewing audience. LCA's licensing policy covers a two-week broadcast period.) The overall cost per student for an ETV broadcast is quite low, but still there are obstacles that prohibit more widespread use of the series.

One problem is that we have too few programs. ETV would like thirteen or twenty-six programs in a series to fill out schedules. Also, ETV objects to inconsistent running times; as with commercial TV, uniform lengths to fit program slots are preferred. (The five "Simply Scientific" films range from eleven to seventeen minutes.) But, as is so often the case in educational matters, lack of funds is the biggest drawback. When making their programming choices, ETV evaluators look at material from two types of sources: commercial producers (such as LCA) and nonprofit producers (which are usually publicly funded educational consortiums). While LCA and most other commercial companies make every attempt to keep licensing fees to a minimum, we cannot compete financially with offerings of tax-exempt groups. ETV evaluators who are carefully watching budgets must often make low cost their first consideration. It's understandable, but unfortunate. Yet the not-for-profit producers are also experiencing budget cuts; to a great extent, we're all suffering together. Now that the National Commission on Excellence in Education has aroused the nation's attention with its report on the ailing state of the U.S. educational system, we hope that funding for educational films will be forthcoming.

While we wait for that budgetary upswing, we are trying to cultivate alternative sources of production that will allow us to keep our prices down and, thus, enable educators to keep using our films. One possibility currently under consideration is a coproduction arrangement with a major videodisc company for more "Simply Scientific" programs. In exchange for underwriting a portion of the production costs, this company would hold exclusive rights to the home market; LCA would retain editorial autonomy and continue to sell the new films to its traditional markets (including educational television).

As we investigate future avenues of production, we're continuing to develop new entries for the series. Some of the subjects we hope to cover are prehistoric animals, fossils, the earth's rotation, the water cycles, and the life cycles of a tree. Teachers have also told us there's a need for simple animated films that explain the workings of the body's major systems, so we're looking into that area as well. There's no shortage of ideas; it's just a question of making them happen during these lean times. We may have to progress a bit more slowly than we'd like. But we will persevere, because the series has proved to fill a definite need in elementary education. Given the recent emphasis on upgrading science education—and with the vigilant efforts of producers, educators, and parents to increase media funding—"Simply Scientific" will continue to introduce serious science to the very young and very curious.

NOTE

1. The idea for this film actually has its roots in my childhood. My family had a summer cottage in the far north woods of Canada. Built on the highest part of an island, it had some fourteen lightning rods—all of which were frighteningly aglow with great balls of fire during big storms. I have never really overcome *my* elemental fear of lightning and thunder, but I thought that a good film on the subject could help kids to get over theirs.

"THE VOYAGE OF THE *MIMI*": AN EXPERIMENT IN SCIENCE EDUCATION

Philip Miller

It is a bright summer morning on board the *Mimi*, a fifty-foot sailboat refitted as a research vessel. Chartered by an ocean research institute, the *Mimi* is sailing the cold waters of the North Atlantic on a six-week mission to track and study humpback whales. Alone on deck, Clement Granville, the boat's captain and owner, stands watch at the ship's wheel, quietly piloting the *Mimi* toward a location where humpbacks have been spotted by a fishing trawler earlier in the day. Far above Captain Granville, perched high in the crosstrees of the main mast, Sally Ruth Cochran, a biology student from Gallaudet College, and C. T. Granville, the captain's eleven-year-old grandson, scan the horizon for signs of the whales.

Below decks, Arthur Spencer, a black teenager from the Bronx, and Rachel Fairbanks, a white teenager from suburban Connecticut, are receiving some last-minute instructions in the techniques of scientific observation and data collection. Once whales are sighted, they will use these techniques to identify and catalogue individual humpbacks. Their instructors are Anne Abrams, an oceanographer, and Ramón Rojas, a marine biologist, who have taken the pair on as their research assistants.

Suddenly, as Ramón reviews a diagram of the physical features used to identify whales, the lesson is interrupted by a cry from the crosstrees. Dropping their diagrams and charts, the scientists and their assistants scramble toward the hatchway. After days of hard preparation and bouts with seasickness, Arthur and Rachel are about to be treated to a seagoing circus performed by nature's largest and most spectacular acrobats. At the same time, they will receive a hurried and harried baptism as cetologists—scientists who study whales and other marine mammals.

Philip Miller *is an associate editor with Knowledge Industry Publications and was a writer and researcher with the Project in Science and Mathematics Education at Bank Street College of Education.*

The *Mimi* sails up to a whale for a closer look in "The Voyage of the *Mimi*." A TV series designed to complement a Bank Street science and math curriculum package. *Photo courtesy of Bank Street College of Education.*

Although the whales and science are real, the captain and his crew are not. They are fictional characters in "The Voyage of the *Mimi*," an innovative educational television series under development at the Bank Street College of Education. The TV drama forms the foundation for a multimedia package of instructional materials, a package designed to support an integrated approach to science and mathematics education in the fourth, fifth, and sixth grades. In addition to the twenty-six-episode TV series, the finished package will include microcomputer software, videodisc materials, a teacher's guide, and student activity books. Bank Street is producing the materials with the assistance of several subcontractors, under a contract with the U.S. Department of Education.

Early in the project, the Bank Street staff faced a number of fundamental production decisions. First, staff members had to determine which of the project's objectives were best met through the TV series, and which were better met through the microcomputer, print, and videodisc materials. Then, before production could begin on the pilot episodes, the staff had to settle on a format, cast of characters, and basic storyline for the TV series.

But why settle on a drama/adventure format? And why such an odd mix of cast members? And why whales? Answering these questions requires a bit of backtracking to the general goals and objectives which were established for the project, and to the important role that research played in the project's production decisions.

With the help of an advisory board, the Bank Street Project in Science and Mathematics Education has established four broad goals for its materials. They are designed to help children understand:

- what it is like to do science and to be scientists;

- how mathematics helps scientists describe and understand natural phenomena;

- how technology, especially computer technology, contributes to scientific inquiry and assists with practical tasks;

- some fundamental concepts in modern science.

In addition to these general goals, the project has a number of smaller, subsidiary objectives. For example, by designing materials that help children understand what it is like to do science, the project also hopes to help students understand how science, math, and the scientific method can help them solve real, everyday problems. Additionally, by designing materials that show children what it is like to be a scientist, the project hopes to help children begin thinking about careers in science, math, and technology. Through its materials, Bank Street wants to foster an interest in science and mathematics among both boys and girls, and among children from all ethnic and economic backgrounds.

By establishing these goals and objectives, the project also set several parameters for the television production decisions that followed. First, to demonstrate what it is like to do science, the television series would have to show scientists on an actual mission or expedition. Second, since several of the project's goals depend on children identifying with the scientists in the TV series, the scientific mission would have to fit within a format that allowed characters to be established and developed in a clear, convincing manner. Finally, both the mission and the format would have to be compelling enough to attract and sustain viewers' interest over twenty-six episodes (the number stipulated in the Department of Education's guidelines.)

With these goals and parameters in mind, the Bank Street staff set about choosing a basic design for the TV series. In an important sense, Bank Street's choice of a dramatic format was a decision to experiment, an intentional break with television tradition. Historically, most TV science shows have been documentaries, programs that present science subject matter in a direct manner, with little extraneous entertainment. In recent years, educational television producers have also developed several science "magazine" shows. Based on a "60 Minutes" model, science magazine programs usually present a wide variety of scientific topics in segments that are introduced and tied together by the comments of a regular host or hosts.

By basing the TV series on a dramatic format, Bank Street knew it was taking a risk. But it was very much a calculated risk, a good bet based on substantial research evidence. In calculating the risks, Bank Street benefited from research that the Children's Television Workshop conducted during the development of its educational programs, especially the science show "3-2-1 Contact." As one part of that research, CTW studied the television viewing preferences of eight-to-twelve-year-olds. Their studies showed that children in this age range clearly prefer dramatic programs over other types of TV fare, including documentaries and magazine shows. Significantly, the CTW research also revealed that children are particularly attracted to dramatic programs that involve characters their own age or slightly older, and that children remember a surprising amount of detail from dramatic presentations (as long as the dramatic context is sufficiently compelling).

From this research, Bank Street knew that a dramatic series probably stood the best chance of attracting and sustaining the attention of young viewers. At the same time, the Bank Street staff recognized that the dramatic format places a number of constraints on the producers of a science series, constraints that limit the amount and character of instructional material the show can contain. With any dramatic series, the demands of the story line come first. To fit with the flow of the story, segments that involve explicit instruction must be brief, and they must be confined to moments in the story when there is a natural need for one character to explain some fact or phenomenon to others. Additionally, once the storyline is set, so are the setting, cast of characters, and science content of the series. If a program breaks with the storyline to introduce extraneous characters or content, or if it turns preachy or didactic, viewers will retaliate by quickly changing the channel.

Because of these constraints, the developers of "3-2-1 Contact" (a group that included Sam Gibbon, who is now the executive director of the Bank Street Project in Science and Mathematics Education) decided against a dramatic format for the CTW program. They went, instead, with a magazine format, a structure that allows producers much more flexibility in selecting and presenting science content. Acknowledging the strength of dramatic presentations, the CTW producers did include a dramatic feature—"The Bloodhound Gang"—as one of the recurring magazine segments in "3-2-1 Contact." Significantly, subsequent research has revealed that "The Bloodhound Gang" is the most popular part of the show with children in the target age range.

Ultimately, Bank Street based its choice of a dramatic format on a review of the available research evidence, on the staff's intuitive sense of television's strengths as an educational medium, and on staff insights into the role that the TV series would play in the project's complete package of instructional materials. For this project, the Bank Street staff felt that television's greatest strength was its ability to present science and scientists in a compelling dramatic context. Within that context, viewers would see science as it naturally occurs—as an ongoing and fundamentally human process, subject to the same sorts of conflicts that complicate and enrich any cooperative enterprise. Just as importantly, the dramatic format would allow students to see young characters engaged in the actual practice of science, rather than simply standing by as observers of an exclusively adult activity. Finally, if they were done well, dramatic programs focusing on young scientists would draw children into a different sort of world, a place where questions are always worth asking and where adults and young people share a natural curiosity and sense of wonder about the world around them.

While recognizing the many benefits of a dramatic format, staff members conceded that a dramatic series would probably not be able to provide the same degree of direct science instruction possible through a documentary or magazine series. But Bank Street also knew that its television series could count on considerable support from the project's microcomputer, print, and videodisc materials. In a final analysis, staff members felt that much of the direct science instruction required to meet the project's educational objectives could be better presented by the classroom teacher using these supplemental materials than by the TV series itself. In other words, within the complete package of project materials, the TV series would primarily serve as a vehicle for stimulating students' natural scientific curiosity, for presenting science in a real and richly human context, and for introducing the science and math concepts that the project's other materials would explore in more depth.

Research also played an important role in another early production decision: the choice of whales as a topic of study for the scientists in the television series. Before making this choice, the Bank Street staff reviewed several other studies conducted by the Children's Television Workshop, studies in which eight- to twelve-year-old children were asked for their reactions to various science topics. In the final ratings, whales consistently ranked at or near the top of children's lists. Significantly, whales were a popular choice with both boys and girls, and with children from a variety of ethnic backgrounds.

In late 1981 and early 1982, the CTW findings were confirmed by Bank Street's own formative research. Through interviews and surveys, the project's research staff found that children had many questions about whales, and that most eight- to twelve-year-old children would be eager to watch a TV drama in which young scientists tried to answer their questions. Once planning for "The Voyage of the *Mimi*" was underway, the Bank Street staff also discovered that whales were a very rich topic of study, a topic that would allow the project to combine elements of biology, oceanography, physics, mathematics, and various other scientific and humanistic disciplines into a single, integrated curriculum.

With these last bits of evidence, the full recommendation of the research staff was in. Roughly summarized, that recommendation read something like this: If you want to produce a science series that attracts and sustains children's interest, and that presents science in a real and convincing context, base it on a drama/adventure format. Have the series focus on whales, and have it include characters who are in your viewers' age range or slightly older. Also, if you want to teach science concepts in depth and detail, plan on producing some supplementary materials. A dramatic series just can't handle that heavy an instructional load on its own.

The unconventional format of the television series is not the only innovative feature of the Bank Street Project in Science and Mathematics Education. To our knowledge, the project is also one of the first in educational television to integrate the production of a TV series with the design and development of microcomputer software. In a sense, the microcomputer software will pick up where the TV series leaves off. As mentioned earlier, the TV series will mainly serve as a means of introducing and stimulating student interest in scientific skills, scientific concepts, and the purpose of scientific inquiry. Picking up on this lead, the microcomputer software will provide exercises and activities that tie in with the TV series, and that allow students to explore the skills and concepts introduced in the series in more depth.

In each of these activities, the Bank Street software will draw upon the computer's capacity for providing interactive, participatory learning experiences. Despite television's many strengths as an educational medium, it does not allow students to take control of the learning sequence. The TV program presents, and the learner responds. With microcomputer programs, students can become active participants in the learning process, and activities can be designed to allow individual students to progress at their own pace. Significantly, computer games and activities can also be designed to simulate the process of scientific inquiry, allowing students to develop and test theories through observation, exploration, and experimentation.

For a project like Bank Street's, television and microcomputers make a powerful pair. Through the television series, young viewers will share in the challenge and adventure of a scientific expedition. During the course of that expedition, viewers will see scientists use many of the observational, measuring, and mathematical skills that are so central to the process of scientific inquiry. Finally, through the microcomputer software, students will have an opportunity to try these skills out for themselves, through activities that tie in with or simulate situations from the TV show.

An example should help show how this interplay between the TV series and the software will work. During "The Voyage of the *Mimi*," the captain and crew use a variety of methods and measuring instruments to chart the ship's position and course. These navigation skills become especially important when the *Mimi* sails near dangerously shallow waters, when the scientists track the humpbacks through their summer feeding grounds, and when a severe storm forces the captain to beach the ship on a remote, deserted island.

The same skills come into play during "Rescue Mission," a microcomputer program developed for Bank Street by Computer Learning Connection, Inc. In "Rescue Mission," teams of children try to locate and reach a whale that is caught in the nets of a fishing trawler (something that occurs quite frequently in the rich fishing waters near Newfoundland). They do this by acquiring and applying basic navigational skills, and by using a variety of simulated navigation instruments similar to those used on board the *Mimi*. In both the TV series and the "Rescue Mission" game, the motivation for learning about and practicing navigation skills is the same: to steer the ship through a successful mission.

Playing "Rescue Mission" has an added benefit. Like the other microcomputer programs being developed for the project, it teaches children something about computers. With "Rescue Mission," students learn how the computer can function as a powerful simulation tool. With the project's other prototype programs, children learn about and test other applications of computer technology. For example, by working with the "Probe" software developed for Bank Street by the Technical Education Research Center, children learn how to use a computer to collect and display data from their physical environments. Additionally, by playing "Whale Search" and "Treasure Hunt," two microcomputer games being developed at Bank Street's Center for Children and Technology, students learn some beginning lessons in programming the computer in LOGO, a powerful computer language designed to be especially accessible to children.

Although the Project in Science and Mathematics Education believes that television and microcomputers make a powerful combination, Bank Street recognizes that many schools still do not have microcomputers. For classrooms that are not equipped with computers, and for classrooms in which a single microcomputer must be shared by a large number of students, the Project in Science and Mathematics Education is developing a variety of noncomputer activities. These activities will be printed in teacher and student guides and, like the other project materials, they will be based on an investigative, hands-on approach to the learning of science.

As part of its contract with the Department of Education, Bank Street is also committed to developing experimental materials on videodisc, an advanced video technology that is just beginning to make its way into America's schools and homes. These experimental materials will include games and activities that expand upon concepts introduced in the TV series, and that take advantage of the videodisc's sophisticated storage and playback features—features that include rapid access to any of the fifty-four thousand frames on each side of the disc, and the various graphic and instructional capabilities that are created when a disc player is interconnected with a microcomputer.

Ultimately, the degree to which Bank Street succeeds in meeting its objectives depends on the degree to which the individual project materials succeed, and on the degree to which the individual materials fit together to form a successful learning package. For the package to succeed, the TV drama must move and motivate children, the microcomputer software must both teach and entertain, and the project's print materials must make the science and math content of the TV series accessible to classrooms with or without computers.

Like many modern educational television projects, the Project in Science and Mathematics Education is conducting extensive field tests of its pilot and prototype materials. So far, those tests indicate that the project's materials are succeeding. The sample episodes from the TV series seem to be capturing and sustaining children's attention, and the sample microcomputer and print materials seem to be teaching what they were designed to teach. Just as importantly, the pieces seem to be fitting together to form a package that motivates students to learn, and that provides teachers with an accessible and effective classroom resource.

Using information obtained from the field tests, Bank Street is revising its pilot television episodes, computer programs, and print guides. Current production schedules call for the complete package of materials to be ready in 1984, with the television series tentatively slotted for a first run that same year. If the finished materials meet with the same response as the pilot versions, Bank Street's gamble will have paid off. The Project in Science and Mathematics Education will have created a learning package that captures the excitement and drama of science, and that capitalizes on the combined strengths of television, computer, and print media.

CONCLUSION

Kim Hays

We repeatedly enlarge our instrumentalities without enlarging our purpose.

Will Durant, historian
(1885–1981)

Both scientists and broadcasters are frequently called upon to help solve society's problems. This book illustrates one such expectation. All of its authors agree that broadcasters and scientists have a joint responsibility to make science more accessible to the general public and, in particular, to young people. Neither group can accomplish this without the cooperation of the other. If scientists scorn television, if TV journalists and producers misrepresent or ignore the sciences, most Americans will remain scientifically illiterate for many years to come.

Both scientists and broadcasters are also frequently blamed for society's problems. That is a trap this book has tried to avoid. Neither television nor science is primarily to blame for our scientific ignorance. It is we, the public, who are chiefly to blame, because we fail to question.

If we teach our children only one thing, we must teach them to ask questions. Or, perhaps more accurately, we should teach them not to stop asking questions. For in fact, children don't have to be taught to question; it is a natural part of their development. Adults, often without meaning to, teach children acquiescence and apathy. Instead, we should foster their interest in science, because the essence of science is the act of asking questions and testing different answers. Physicist Niels Bohr said, "Every sentence I utter must be understood not as an affirmation, but as a question." Animal behaviorist Konrad Lorenz put it another way when he said, "Truth in science can be defined as the working hypothesis best suited to open the way to the next better one." Stifling a young child's impulse to question and stifling his or her interest in science are comparable, since the answers to most of the endless questions children ask about everything around them are rooted in science.

I am not suggesting that we should encourage children to make chattering nuisances of themselves from morning till night so they will all grow up to be scientists. My goal is neither a country full of undisciplined children nor one full of scientists. What we want, ideally, is a country full of people with enough background in science, enough interest in science, and enough of the questioning spirit that the study of science imparts to be able to criticize science—or to praise it, when praise is due. But we must at least be able to keep

171

an eye on where science and technology are taking us, to make sure that it is where we want to go. And we must be able to understand and try to avert some of the less than desirable consequences of the requests we make of science. If we demand cheap electricity, convenience foods, disposable products, and endless mass-produced consumer goods of all sorts without thinking through the problems of their creation, then we must not act surprised when we get, in addition to these wonders, nuclear wastes, chemical additives, litter, and terrible pollution.

How is the American public going to get to the stage of scientific literacy that will allow its members to ask the right questions? By demanding and then supporting better science education in the schools for our children, better science education in the media (especially television) for adults and children alike, and, in particular, better science education for journalists. Until a larger portion of the public has learned to be both more understanding and more critical of scientists and their work, journalists must do the criticizing for us. A journalist whose ignorance of science causes him or her to parrot everything stated by a scientist without question is doing readers, listeners, or viewers almost as much of a disservice as the journalist whose ignorance of science causes him or her to make major mistakes in reporting.

Most of these changes will not take place until the federal government puts sufficient funding into science education of every kind. Corporate attempts to improve scientific literacy through classroom materials and TV series deserve our applause, but industry dollars will inevitably buy an industry perspective. Federal tax dollars have strings attached to them, too, but not as many. Those of us who believe that scientific literacy is important must be willing to put our money where our mouths are, and must tell our government representatives to do the same. Scientists, in particular, must speak out in support of federal action.

But, one might well ask, why should scientists want to help the public learn more about science, if the result is going to be that the more we understand, the more we question what they are doing? There are, in fact, many scientists who don't want to be bothered with a layperson's critical, or even sympathetic, questions. Luckily, there are other scientists who see that the discrepancy between the vastness of society's means and meanness of its purposes will not be changed without education. They want to promote public education in the sciences because they want a public—and a government—that will not misuse their discoveries.

In his *Advice to a Young Scientist*, Peter Medawar writes:

The role I envisage for the scientist is that which may be described as "scientific meliorism." A meliorist is simply one who believes the world can be made a better place.... Those with enough hopefulness in their makeup will go along with the belief

... that the pursuit of universal learning 'to be acquired and applied to the benefit of all men for the common good' is truly ... the way of light.

Even scientific meliorists must operate within the same volatile, political society as the rest of us; as long as the lay world remains in darkness, they will find it exceedingly difficult to follow the way of light. It is to scientists' benefit to help us understand and evaluate them, so that they will be able to do the best work they are capable of doing. It is to our benefit to educate ourselves about science, so that we can use scientists' work to the world's best advantage.

APPENDIXES
Paula Rohrlick
TELEVISION SERIES

This selected list of network, cable, local, syndicated, and instructional programs about science is for informational purposes only and is not meant to indicate endorsement by Action for Children's Television. The dates given signify the first time each series was shown. Note that many of the network programs are no longer being aired.

COMMERCIAL BROADCASTING, PUBLIC BROADCASTING, AND CABLE SERIES

Alive and Well
USA Cable Network, 120 min.
October 5, 1981–

A daily health, nutrition, and exercise series sponsored by Bristol-Myers and produced by DBA Television, Inc., Hollywood, CA.

Animals Animals Animals
ABC, 30 min.
September 12, 1976–November 8, 1981

A Sunday morning series for children that focused on a different animal each week, produced by ABC News, New York, and narrated by Hal Linden.

The Ascent of Man
PBS, 60 min.
January 7, 1975–April 1, 1975

A series about how the human race developed and how scientific discoveries influenced the growth of civilization, hosted by Dr. Jacob Bronowski. The series was produced by Time-Life Films, New York, and BBC.

The Body Human
CBS, 60 min. and 30 min.
March 16, 1977–

A series of informational specials about aspects of the human body, produced by The Tomorrow Entertainment/Medcom Co., New York.

The Body in Question
PBS, 60 min.
September 30, 1980–December 23, 1980

A thirteen-part weekly series about the human body, written and hosted by Dr. Jonathan Miller. KCET, Los Angeles, and BBC coproduced the programs, which were funded by KCET and Hoffman-LaRoche and are distributed by Films Inc., Wilmette, IL.

The Body Works
syndicated, 30 min.
August 1979–June 1982

A thirteen-episode series of children's programs dealing with the functions of the human body, hosted by Dr. Timothy Johnson and three twelve-year-old assistants. It was produced by WCVB, Boston, and syndicated by Metromedia Producers Corp., Boston.

Cable Health Network
basic cable service, 24 hours daily
June 30, 1982–February 1, 1984

Paula Rohrlick is the resource director for Action for Children's Television.

An advertiser-supported cable network with headquarters in New York that offered over twenty series on health, science, and life-style topics.

The Computer Programme
PBS, 30 min.
April 16, 1983–June 18, 1983

A series of ten weekly programs produced by BBC that explain computers and their functions. The PBS broadcast is underwritten by Acorn Computer Corp. of Woburn, MA. The series is distributed by Films Inc., Wilmette, IL.

Connections
PBS, 60 min.
September 30, 1979–December 2, 1979

A ten-part documentary series on the history of technology, coproduced by BBC and Time-Life Films, New York. It was written and narrated by James Burke and funded by AT&T.

Cosmos
PBS, 60 min.
September 28, 1980–December 21, 1980

A thirteen-part series about astronomy and space exploration written by Adrian Malone and Dr. Carl Sagan and hosted by Sagan. It was produced by KCET, Los Angeles, and Carl Sagan Productions, and it is distributed by Films Inc., Wilmette, IL.

Discover: The World of Science
syndicated, 60 min.
January 1982–

A series of specials about the latest in scientific development and research, and how they affect our daily lives. Some of the specials have been sponsored by Atari, Inc. The programs are produced by The Chedd-Angier Production Co., Inc., Boston, in association with *Discover* magazine, and distributed by Young and Rubicam, Inc., New York.

Healthbeat
syndicated, 30 min.
October 1981–

A weekly health magazine series hosted by Dr. Timothy Johnson and produced by Metromedia Producers Corp., Boston.

How About . . .
syndicated, 80 sec.
April 1979–

A series of 208 science news inserts produced by the Mr. Wizard Studio, Canoga Park, CA, and hosted by Don Herbert (Mr. Wizard). The segments are funded by the National Science Foundation and General Motors and distributed by King Features Entertainment, New York.

Innovation
WNET(New York), 30 min.
April 15, 1983–July 22, 1983; Fall 1983–

A weekly science and technology series hosted by Jim Hartz that focuses on major research advances and the implications of scientific breakthroughs. Funding has been provided by various foundations and companies, including Bell Laboratories, AT&T, Johnson & Johnson, and the Robert Wood Johnson Foundation.

Life on Earth
PBS, 60 min.
January 12, 1982–April 6, 1982

A thirteen-part series about the evolutionary process from single-cell creatures to humans, hosted by David Attenborough and underwritten by Mobil Corp. It was produced by BBC in association with Warner Bros.

Marie Curie
PBS, 60 min.
October 11, 1978–November 8, 1978

A five-part series about the life and work of the famous woman scientist, starring Jane Lapotaire. The series was coproduced by the BBC and Time-Life Films, New York and presented by WCET, Cincinnati.

Mr. Wizard
NBC, 30 min.
March 3, 1951–June 27, 1965; September 4, 1971–September 2, 1972

An educational program for children, demonstrating scientific experiments, starring Don Herbert as Mr. Wizard.

Mr. Wizard's World
Nickelodeon, 30 min.
October 3, 1983–

A magazine-format show aimed at children and adolescents that features science experiments. It stars Don Herbert as Mr. Wizard, and is produced by Nickelodeon.

National Geographic Specials
CBS/ABC/PBS, 60 min.
1965–1973 (CBS)
1973–1975 (ABC)
1975– (PBS)

A series of documentary specials about scientific subjects, produced by the National Geographic Society and WQED, Pittsburgh, with a grant from Gulf Oil Corp.

Nature
PBS, 60 min.
October 10, 1982–January 2, 1983

Thirteen weekly programs tracing the history of the study of animal behavior, produced by WNET, New York.

New! Animal World
The Disney Channel, 30 min.
April 18, 1983–

A daily look at animals around the world, hosted by Bill Burrud and produced by Bill Burrud Productions, Los Angeles.

Nova
PBS, 60 min.
March 3, 1974–

A weekly documentary series about science, technology, and medicine. Some of the programs were first shown on the BBC science series "Horizon"; the others were produced by WGBH, Boston. Funding is provided by public television stations, The Arthur Vining Davis Foundations, and Johnson & Johnson.

Omni: The New Frontier
syndicated, 30 min.
September 1981–February 1982

A magazine-format show that examined how scientific discoveries will affect our future. It was produced and syndicated by Omni Productions, New York, in association with *Omni Magazine*.

Powerhouse
PBS, 30 min.
December 12, 1982–January 21, 1983

A daily children's and family action/adventure series that provided information about physical and mental health. Funded by a grant from the U.S. Department of Education, the series was produced by the Educational Film Center, Annandale, VA, and is distributed by TeleWorld Inc., New York.

The Scheme of Things
The Disney Channel, 30 min.
April 18, 1983–

A daily, scientific-adventure, documentary series for family audiences, hosted by Mark Shaw and produced by Power/Rector Productions, San Francisco.

Schoolhouse Rock
ABC, 3 min.
January 1973–

Animated, musical educational segments produced by Newall and Yohe, Inc., New York. The Saturday morning series includes "Science Rock," "Multiplication Rock," and "Scooter Computer and Mr. Chips."

The Search for Solutions
PBS, 60 min.
June 10, 17, and 24, 1980

A special three-part series about scientists and their work, produced by Playback Associates, New York, and hosted and narrated by Stacy Keach. The programs were funded by Phillips Petroleum, which distributes them for classroom use.

Slim Goodbody's Top 40 Health Hits
Nickelodeon
September, 1982–

A series of twenty-six one-minute episodes consisting of songs for young people about good health and nutrition habits, produced by Sheryl Johnston Communications, Chicago,

and underwritten by Kraft, Inc. The series has also appeared on CBS's "Captain Kangaroo" in a longer form.

Spaces
PBS, 30 min.
January 30, 1984–March 5, 1984

A six-part weekly science magazine series targeted to minority children, produced by WETA, Washington, D.C., with InterAmerica Research Associates and funded by the U.S. Department of Education and the Alcoa Foundation. It highlights the accomplishments of minority scientists in order to encourage minority children to consider careers in science.

Synthesis
PBS, 60 min. and 30 min.
November 8, 1977–

An occasional series of documentary specials exploring the scientific and technical aspects of public policy issues. The specials are produced by KPBS, San Diego, and funded by the National Science Foundation.

3-2-1 Contact
PBS, 30 min.
January 14, 1980–April 11, 1980 (Season I);
October 17, 1983–January 13, 1984 (Season II)

A daily introduction to science and technology in a magazine format for eight- to twelve-year-olds, produced by Children's Television Workshop, New York. Both seasons were funded by the National Science Foundation, the U.S. Department of Education, and the Corporation for Public Broadcasting. Season I was also funded by United Technologies

Corporation and Children's Television Workshop.

The Undersea World of Jacques Cousteau
ABC/syndicated, 60 min.
January 8, 1968–June 13, 1976 (ABC)
1976– (syndicated)

A series of documentary specials about the underwater explorations of Cousteau and his crew of marine biologists, produced by The Cousteau Society and Metromedia Producers Corp., Los Angeles, and distributed by Metromedia Producers Corp., Boston.

The Voyage of the *Mimi*
PBS, 30 min.
Summer 1984

A thirteen-episode weekly adventure series for nine- to twelve-year-olds about the study of whales. The programs were produced as part of a science curriculum package by Peace River Films, Inc., for Bank Street College of Education, New York, under a contract with the U.S. Department of Education.

Walter Cronkite's Universe
CBS, 30 min.
June 27, 1979; July 12, 1980–August 2, 1980; June 21, 1981–September 8, 1981; June 8, 1982–September 14, 1982

A weekly science magazine series anchored by Walter Cronkite that was produced by CBS News and aired during the summers. Reports examined topics in science and technology.

The Weather Channel
basic cable service, 24 hours daily
May 2, 1982–

Daily round-the-clock weather programming, with national, regional, and local forecasts and weather-related features.

What Will They Think of Next?
Nickelodeon, 30 min.
April 1980–

A magazine-format series for families, produced by Science International, Toronto, about new scientific developments.

Wild Wild World of Animals
syndicated, 30 min.
1973–

A documentary series on animal life narrated by William Conrad. It was produced by Time-Life Films and is distributed by Ganaway Enterprises, Atlanta.

Wild America
PBS, 30 min.
October 14, 1982–December 16, 1982; October 13, 1983–December 15, 1983

A documentary series about American wildlife produced by Marty Stouffer Productions Ltd., Aspen.

Wild Kingdom
NBC/syndicated, 30 min.
January 6, 1963–April 11, 1971 (NBC); 1971– (syndicated)

Weekly documentary films about animal life produced by Don Meier Productions, Chicago, and sponsored by Mutual of Omaha.

INSTRUCTIONAL SERIES ABOUT SCIENCE AND RELATED TOPICS FOR YOUNG PEOPLE

Agency for Instructional Television (AIT)
Located in Bloomington, IN, AIT develops and distributes educational programs for classroom use.

ALL ABOUT YOU
ANIMAL BEHAVIOR SERIES
ANIMALS AND SUCH
BIOSCOPE
COMMUNITY OF LIVING THINGS
CONRAD
DISCOVERING
EXPLORERS UNLIMITED
FIGURE OUT
FIRST FILMS ON SCIENCE
HANDS ON
THE INSIDE STORY WITH SLIM
 GOODBODY
IT FIGURES
JANE GOODALL: STUDIES OF THE
 CHIMPANZEE
LANDSAT: SATELLITE FOR ALL
 SEASONS
MATH COUNTRY
MATH MATTERS
MATHWAYS
MATH WISE
MATTER AND MOTION
MEASUREMETRIC
METRIFY OR PETRIFY
NATURAL SCIENCE SPECIALS
SEARCH FOR LIFE
SEE 'N' TELL
SKILLS ESSENTIAL TO LEARNING,
 PHASE II–MATHEMATICS
SOUP-TO-NUTS
TERRA: OUR WORLD
UNIVERSE AND I
WEATHER MATRIX

WHATABOUT
WHY?
YOU, ME, AND TECHNOLOGY
ZOO ZOO ZOO

Children's Television International (CTI)
CTI, located in Springfield, VA, produces and distributes educational and instructional TV series.

ADVENTURE OF THE MIND: A
 SERIES ON PERSONAL
 COMPUTING
DRAGONS, WAGONS AND WAX
L-4

Great Plains National Instructional Television Library (GPN)
Headquartered in Lincoln, NE, GPN distributes instructional programs for classroom or general use.

BASIC TRAINING
DR. ALLHART AND PATIENCE
EXPLORA LA CIENCIA
HIGH FEATHER
INFINITY FACTORY
LITTLE COMPUTERS ... SEE HOW
 THEY RUN
MAINLY MATH
MAP AND GLOBE SKILLS
MATH FACTORY
MATH MISSION 2
MEASURE TO MEASURE
MEASURE UP
THE MEASURING SHOW
METRIC MARMALADE
THE METRIC SYSTEM
MULLIGAN STEW
ODYSSEY

SCIENCE IS SEARCHING
SEARCH FOR SCIENCE
SHAPES OF GEOMETRY
STUDIO M
TELL ME WHAT YOU SEE
UNDERSTANDING OUR WORLD
WHAT ON EARTH?

Learning Corporation of America (LCA)
LCA, located in New York, distributes educational and entertainment films and videocassettes for young people.

ANIMALS AND PLANTS OF
  NORTH AMERICA
CHILDREN'S ECOLOGY
ENVIRONMENTAL SCIENCES
THE REAL WORLD OF INSECTS
SIMPLY SCIENTIFIC

TVOntario
TVOntario is the television service of The Ontario Educational Communications Authority, with offices in Toronto and Dallas. It produces and distributes educational materials for classroom or general use.

THE BODY WORKS
CHALLENGE TO SCIENCE
EUREKA!

FAST FORWARD 1
FAST FORWARD 2
LANDSCAPE OF GEOMETRY
LIKE NO OTHER PLACE
MATH PATROL 2
MATH PATROL 3
MATHEMATICAL CONCEPTS
MATHEMATICAL RELATIONSHIPS
MATHMAKERS 1
MATHMAKERS 2
NORTH AMERICA: GROWTH OF A
  CONTINENT
THE PLANET OF MAN
THE SCIENCE ALLIANCE
TWO PLUS YOU (MATH PATROL 1)
THE WHITE INFERNO

Western Instructional Television
Western Instructional Television, located in Los Angeles, produces and distributes televised instruction to be used by state departments of education, public broadcasting stations, state ETV networks, and individual school districts.

EXPLORING THE WORLD OF
  SCIENCE
PROFESSOR JULIUS SUMNER
  MILLER
UNCOMMON MEN AND GREAT
  IDEAS

BOOKS AND ARTICLES

This is a selected list of books and articles about science. It is divided into four categories: public attitudes toward science and scientists; learning about science; women and minorities in the sciences; and science and the media.

PUBLIC ATTITUDES TOWARD SCIENCE AND SCIENTISTS

Asimov, Isaac. "What's Fueling the Popular Science Explosion?" *Saturday Review*, August 1980, 23–26.

Carey, William D. "Science and Public Understanding." *Science* 204 (1979): 797.

Chambers, David Wade. "Stereotypic Images of the Scientist: The Draw-A-Scientist Test." *Science Education* 67 (1983):255–265.

Dismukes, Key. "What Should Society Expect from Scientists?" *The Bulletin of the Atomic Scientists* 35 (November 1979):19–21.

Goodell, Rae. *The Visible Scientists*. Boston:Little, Brown and Company, 1977.

Hanley, John W. "How Can 'Good' Science Prevail in Shaping of Public Opinion?" *Science Digest*, August 1980, 49–51.

"Informing the Public: Why Bother?" *SIPIscope*, January/February 1982, 1–7.

La Follette, Marcel Chotkowki, comp. *Citizen and Science Almanac and Annotated Bibliography*. Bloomington, Ind.: The Poynter Center on American Institutions, Indiana University, 1977.

Miller, Jon D. "Scientific Literacy: A Conceptual and Empirical Review." *Daedalus* 112 (Spring 1983): 29–48.

Miller, Jon D.; Prewitt, Kenneth; and Pearson, Robert. *The Attitudes of the U.S. Public Toward Science and Technology*. Chicago: National Opinion Research Center, University of Chicago, July 1980.

Miller, Jon D.; Suchner, Robert W.; and Voelker, Alan M. *Citizenship in an Age of Science: Changing Attitudes Among Young Adults*. New York: Pergamon Press, 1980.

"Needed: More Close Encounters!" *Science Digest*, April 1979, 42–43.

Rosenfeld, Albert. "How Anxious Should Science Make Us?" *Saturday Review*, 9 June 1979, 16–21.

Trachtman, Leon E. "The Public Understanding of Science Effort: A Critique." *Science, Technology, and Human Values* 6 (Summer 1981): 10.

Walsh, John. "Public Attitude Toward Science is Yes, But—" *Science* 215 (1982): 270–272.

Yankelovich, Daniel. "Changing Public Attitudes to Science and the Quality of Life." *Science, Technology, and Human Values* 7 (Spring 1982): 23–29.

LEARNING ABOUT SCIENCE

Abruscato, Joseph. *Teaching Children Science.* Englewood Cliffs, N.J.: Prentice-Hall, 1982.

Champagne, Audrey B.; and Klepper, Leopold E. "Science Teaching: Theory and Classroom Practice." *Education Digest,* March 1981, 42–44.

"The Education Gap." *Scientific American,* August 1982, 64–65.

Education in the Sciences: A Developing Crisis. Washington, D.C.: American Association for the Advancement of Science, April 1982.

Gale, G. "I Ain't A-Gonna Dry Lab No More, Or, Some Thoughts on the Curious But Significant Relation Between Science Education and the Philosophy of Science." *Journal of College Science Teaching* 10 (1981): 342–45.

Gallagher, James J.; and Yager, Robert E. "Science Educators' Perceptions of Problems Facing Science Education: A Report of Five Surveys." *Journal of Research in Science Teaching* 18 (1981): 505–14.

Gega, Peter C. *Science in Elementary Education.* New York: John Wiley and Sons, 1982.

Goldberg, L. "Elementary School Science: Learning How to Learn." *Science and Children* 20 (April 1982): 10–11.

Good, Ronald G. *How Children Learn Science: Conceptual Development and Implications for Teaching.* New York: Macmillan, 1977.

Greenleaf, Warren T. "Uncle Sam Wants You: New Federal Science Improvement Program Aims to Recruit Principals." *Principal,* September 1982, 18–21.

Holt, Bess-Gene. *Science with Young Children.* Washington, D.C.: National Association for the Education of Young Children, 1977.

Hurd, P. DeH. "State of Precollege Education in Mathmetics and Science." *Science Education* 67 (1983): 57–67.

Hurd, P. DeH.; Robinson, J. T.; McConnell, M.C.; and Ross, N.M., Jr. *The Status of Middle School and Junior High School Science.* 2 vols. Louisville, Co.: Center for Educational Research and Evaluation, 1981.

Kyle, W. C., Jr. "Should Scientific Creation and the Science of Evolution Be Taught with Equal Emphasis?" *Journal of Research in Science Teaching* 17 (1980): 519–27.

Mallow, Jeffry V. *Science Anxiety: Fear of Science and How to Overcome It.* New York: Van Nostrand Reinhold, 1982.

McGrath, Ellie. "Low-Tech Teaching Blues: Crisis in the Math and Science Classroom." *Time,* 27 December 1982, 67.

Mechling, Kenneth R. "Taking Charge: How Principals Can Improve School Science Programs." *Principal*, January 1983, 16–21.

Mechling, Kenneth R.; and Oliver, Donna L. "The 4th R: Science, Stepchild of the Elementary Curriculum." *Principal*, November 1982, 28–37.

Medawar, Peter B. *Advice to a Young Scientist.* New York: Harper and Row, 1979.

Moravcsik, Michael J. "Creativity in Science Education." *Science Education* 65 (1981): 221–27.

National Academy of Sciences. *Science and Mathematics Education in the Schools: Report of a Convocation.* Washington, D.C.: National Academy Press, 1982.

National Commission on Excellence in Education. *A Nation at Risk: The Imperative for Educational Reform.* Washington, D.C.: U.S. Government Printing Office, April 1983.

Neuman, Donald B. "Elementary Science for All Children: An Impossible Dream or a Reachable Goal?" *Science and Children*, March 1981, 4–6.

Office of Scientific and Engineering Personnel and Education. *Science and Engineering Education: Data and Information.* Washington, D.C.: National Science Foundation, 1982.

Orlich, Donald C. "Remembering Sputnik, Or, Whatever Happened to School Science?" *The National Elementary Principal*, January 1980, 67–72.

Postman, Neil. "Engaging Students in the Great Conversation." *Phi Delta Kappan* 64 (January 1983): 310–316.

Rapoport, Roger. "Why Johnny Hates Science." *Science 81*, October 1981, 36–39.

Renner, John; Brumby, Margaret; and Shepherd, Debbie L. "Why Are There No Dinosaurs in Oklahoma?" *The Science Teacher*, December 1981, 22–24.

Rowe, Mary Budd. *Teaching Science as Continuous Inquiry.* 2nd ed., rev. New York: McGraw-Hill, 1978.

Saterstrom, Mary H., ed. *Educators Guide to Free Science Materials.* Randolph, Wis.: Educators Progress Service, 1982.

Science and Education (special issue). *Science for the People*, November/December 1979.

Science Education: The Forgotten Imperative (special issue). *The National Elementary Principal*, January 1980.

Shymansky, James; Kyle, William, Jr.; and Alport, Jennifer. "Alphabet Soup Science." *The Science Teacher*, November 1982, 49–53.

Stake, R.E.; and Easley, J. *Case Studies in Science Education.* Washington, D.C.: Government Printing Office, 1978.

"The Status of Science Education." *Education Digest*, November 1982, 36–39.

Thomas, Lewis. "The Art of Teaching Science." *New York Times Magazine*, 14 March 1982, 89–91.

Tobias, Sheila. *Overcoming Math Anxiety.* Boston. Houghton Mifflin, 1978.

Today's Problems: Tomorrow's Crises. Washington, D.C.: National Science Board Commission on Precollege Education in Mathematics, Science, and Technology, October 18, 1982.

Weiss, I.R. *Report of the 1977 National Survey of Science, Mathematics, and Social Sciences Education.* Washington, D.C.: Government Printing Office, 1977.

Yager, R.E. "Is Science a Bunch of Boring Facts?" *The Science Teacher*, April 1982, 41–42.

Yager, Robert; Hoffstein, Ari; and Lunetta, Vincent. "Science Education Attuned to Social Issues: Challenges for the 1980s." *The Science Teacher*, December 1981, 12–13.

Zacharias, Jerrold R. "The Case of the Missing Scientists." *The National Elementary Principal*, January 1980, 14–17.

WOMEN AND MINORITIES IN THE SCIENCES

Asimov, Isaac. "Wanted: Half of the Human Race to Solve Life-or-Death Crisis." *Science Digest*, March 1980, 12–15.

Branscomb, Lewis M. "Women in Science." *Science*, 24 August 1979, 251.

Briscoe, Anne. "Diary of a Mad Feminist Chemist." *International Journal of Women's Studies* 4 (1981): 420–430.

Briscoe, Anne; and Pfafflin, Sheila M., eds. "Expanding the Role of Women in the Sciences." *Annals of the New York Academy of Sciences* 323 (1979).

Cole, Jonathan R. *Fair Science: Women in the Scientific Community.* New York: Free Press, 1979.

Committee on the Education and Employment of Women in Science and Engineering. *Women Scientists in Industry and Government: How Much Progress in the 1970s?* Washington, D.C.: National Academy Press, 1980.

Emberlin, Diane D. *Contribution of Women: Science.* Minneapolis: Dillon Press, 1977.

Goldreich, Gloria; and Goldreich, Esther. *What Can She Be? A Scientist.* New York: Holt, Rinehart and Winston, 1981.

Haber, Louis. *Black Pioneers of Science and Invention.* New York: Harcourt Brace Jovanovich, 1970.

Haber, Louis. *Women Pioneers of Science.* rev. ed. New York: Harcourt Brace Jovanovich, 1979.

Hayman, Diana. "Minority Institutions Science Improvement Program." *American Education*, August/September 1981, 37–38.

"Helping Women in Physics Succeed." *Physics Today*, September 1980, 144.

"Impact Spotlights Bias Against Women Scientists." *UNESCO Courier*, September 1980, 3–4.

Jensen, Cheryl. "Going to the Source: Minority Science Students Spend a Summer in the Inner Sanctums of Basic Research." *American Education*, March 1981, 18–23.

Kistiakowsky, Vera. "Women in Physics: Unnecessary, Injurious, and Out of Place?" *Physics Today*, February 1980, 32–40.

Kogelmen, Stanley; Forman, Susan; and Asch, Jan. "Math Anxiety: Help for Minority Students." *American Educator*, Fall 1981, 30–32.

Kreinberg, Nancy. *I'm Madly in Love with Electricity and Other Comments About Their Work by Women in Science and Engineering*. Berkeley, Calif.: University of California Press, 1977.

Mendeloff, John. "Women Still on the Short End of Science." *Technology Review*, May 1980, 86.

"Minorities Not Encouraged to Pursue Science Careers." *Jet*, 28 May 1981, 24.

National Science Foundation. *Women and Minorities in Science and Engineering*. Washington, D.C.: Government Printing Office, 1977.

Noble, Iris. *Contemporary Women Scientists of America*. New York: Julian Messner, 1979.

Perl, Teri. *Math Equals: Biographies of Women Mathematicians*. Reading, Mass.: Addison-Wesley, 1978.

Rossiter, Margaret W. *Women Scientists in America: Struggles and Strategies to 1940*. Baltimore: The Johns Hopkins University Press, 1982.

Sayre, Anne. *Rosalind Franklin and DNA*. New York: W.W. Norton, 1975.

Shapley, Deborah. "Obstacles to Women in Science." *Impact of Science on Society* 25 (1975): 115–123.

Smith, Walter S.; and Stroup, Kala M. *Science Career Exploration for Women*. Washington, D.C.: National Science Teachers Association, 1978.

Vetter, Betty M. "Working Women Scientists and Engineers." *Science*, 4 January 1980, 28–34.

Women in Science: A Man's World (special issue). *Impact of Science on Society* 25:2 (1975).

"Women—Minorities in Science and Technology." *Science*, 9 October 1981, 137.

SCIENCE AND THE MEDIA

"The AIP in 1981." *Physics Today*, July 1982, 25–32.

Alexander, George. "Don Herbert: Gee Wiz!" *SciQuest*, May/June 1981, 21–23.

American Association for the Advancement of Science. *Science on Television.* Washington, D.C.: American Association for the Advancement of Science, 1975. AAAS Miscellaneous Publication #74-17.

Anglada, A.; and Martinez-Perez, L. *A Children's Television Series About Science and Technology: Considerations on the Hispanic Audience.* New York: Children's Television Workshop, 1979.

"Believe It or Not? *Contact* Looks at Science on TV." *3-2-1 Contact,* November 1979, 4–7.

Bennett, William. "Science Goes Glossy." *The Sciences* 19 (September 1979): 10–15, 22.

_____. "Science Hits the Newsstand." *Columbia Journalism Review,* January/February 1981, 53–57.

Broad, William J. "Science Magazines: The Second Wave Rolls In." *Science,* 15 January 1982, 272–273.

Bronowski, Jacob. *The Ascent of Man.* Boston: Little, Brown and Company, 1974.

Burke, James. *Connections.* Boston: Little, Brown and Company, 1979.

Burrows, William E. "Science Meets the Press: Bad Chemistry." *The Sciences* 20 (April 1980): 15.

Chen, M.; Clarke, H.; and Katz, B.M. *3-2-1 Contact, A TV Series on Science and Technology for Children 8–12: Test Show Evaluation.* New York: Children's Television Workshop, 1979.

Cook, Bruce. "Recruiting Support for Science." *Science Digest,* September 1980, 8–15.

Dale, Donna, "Television Reporting: Student Style." *Science and Children,* February 1981, 8–11.

Davis, Harold L. "Physics on TV." *Physics Today,* August 1980, 96.

Davis, Monte. "Television: Walter Cronkite's *Universe.*" *Discovery,* August 1981, 82.

Dean, Joan F. "Between *2001* and *Star Wars.*" *Journal of Popular Film and Television* 7:1 (1978): 32–41.

Dunwoody, Sharon; and Scott, Byron T. "Scientists as Mass Media Sources." *Journalism Quarterly* 59:1 (Spring 1982): 52–59.

Farago, Peter. *Science and the Media.* London: Oxford University Press, 1976.

Garfield, Eugene. "*Scientific American*—One Hundred and Thirty-six Years of Science Journalism." *Current Contents* 21 (25 May 1981): 5–11.

Gerbner, George; Gross, Larry; Morgan, Michael; and Signorielli, Nancy. "Health and Medicine on TV." *The New England Journal of Medicine* 305 (1981): 901–904.

_____. "Scientists on the TV Screen." *Society,* May/June 1981, 41–44.

_____. *Television's Contribution to Public Understanding of Science: A Pilot*

Project. Washington, D.C.: National Science Foundation, 1980. Report to the National Science Foundation.

Gerbner, George; Morgan, Michael; and Signorielli, Nancy. "Programming Health Portrayals—What Viewers See, Say, and Do." *Television and Behavior: Ten Years of Scientific Progress and Implications for the Eighties, Vol. 2: Technical Reviews.* David Pearl, Lorraine Bouthilet, and Joyce Lazar, eds. 291–307. Rockville, Md.: National Institute of Mental Health, 1982.

Gladstone, Josephine. "Commentary: Remarks on the Portrayal of Scientists." *Science, Technology, and Human Values* 5 (Summer 1980): 4–9.

Goldberg, Carey. "Who Knows Best—The Doctor or the Reporter?" *TV Guide,* 27 November 1982, 43–46.

Goldman, Ronald J.; Gingras, Richard L.; Dordick, Herbert S.; and Levine, Larry S. *A Study of the Potential of Science Programming on Pay Television.* Washington, D.C.: National Science Foundation, 1980.

Goodfield, June. *Reflections on Science and the Media.* Washington, D.C.: American Association for the Advancement of Science, 1981.

Greenberg, Daniel. "Scientific Magazines Bursting Out All Over." *Science and Government Report,* 15 January 1979, 1–2.

Henig, Robin Morantz. "NSF Public Television Project Brings Science Policy to the People." *BioScience* 29 (February 1979): 125–26.

Jerome, Fred. "The Great Science and Technology Bazaar." *Technology Review,* May/June 1981, 16–18.

————. "Whatever Happened to the Science Media Boom?" *Technology Review,* January 1983, 12.

Judson, Horace Freeland. *The Search For Solutions.* New York: Holt, Rinehart and Winston, 1980.

Kagan, Norman. "Science on TV: Patent Office in an Insane Asylum." *Sightlines,* Fall 1981, 15–19.

Katz, Barbara Myerson. "CTW's New Science Series: The Role of Formative Research." *Televisions* 7: 2/3 (1980): 24–31.

Kendig, Frank. "Kids and Science: Making Contact at Last." *Television Quarterly* 17 (Spring 1980): 73–76.

Kirsch, Jeffrey W. "On a Strategy for Using the Electronic Media to Improve the Public Understanding of Science and Technology." *Science, Technology, and Human Values* 4 (Spring 1979): 52–58.

Klein, Judy. "The Medium Gets a Message." *Science News,* 2 June 1979, 364–365.

La Follette, Marcel Chotkowski. "Commentary: Science on Japanese Public Television—An Adaptable Model for the U.S.?" *Science, Technology, and Human Values* 4 (Spring 1979): 59–65.

_____. "Science on Television: Influences and Strategies." *Daedalus* 3 (Fall 1982): 183–197.

_____. "Wizards, Villains, and Other Scientists: Science Content of Television for Children." Unpublished study, July 1978. Copies can be obtained from the author at Room E51-008, MIT, Cambridge, Mass. 02139.

Lakoff, Sanford A. "Grass Roots TV Looks at Science and Public Policy." *The Bulletin of the Atomic Scientists*, December 1978, 51–54.

Le Guin, Ursula. "The Lathe of Heaven." *Horizon*, January 1980, 32–36.

MacKenzie, Robert. "Review: Animals Animals Animals." *TV Guide*, 5 April 1980, 48.

_____. "Review: Connections." *TV Guide*, 6 October 1979, 32.

_____. "Review: Life on Earth." *TV Guide*, 27 February 1982, 26.

_____. "Review: 3-2-1 Contact." *TV Guide*, 6 December 1980, 64.

Mason, Timothy. "Television: Dr. Miller's Deft Dissection." *Saturday Review*, September 1980, 92–93.

Meyer, Alfred. "The Polestar of Public TV." *Science 83*, April 1983, 88.

Meyers, Bill. "The Advance of Science." *Washington Journalism Review*, November 1981, 36–37.

Miller, Jonathan. *The Body in Question*. New York: Random House, 1979.

Morrison, Philip; and Morrison, Phylis. "Science Books for Children: A Working Collection." *The National Elementary Principal*, January 1980, 73–76.

Morrow, James. "Is There a Cure for Scientific Illiteracy?" *Media and Methods*, October 1980, 23.

Morton, Miriam. "The Incredible, Yet Obvious: Science for Young Viewers in the USSR. An Interview with Sergei P. Kapitza." *Television and Children*, Summer 1982, 43–52.

Nunn, Clyde Z. "Readership and Coverage of Science and Technology in Newspapers." *Journalism Quarterly* 56 (Spring 1979): 27–30.

O'Connor, John J. "Putting 'Cosmos' into Perspective." *The New York Times*, 14 December 1980, D36.

On Public Communication of Science and Technology (Special issue). *Science, Technology, and Human Values* 36 (Summer 1981).

Rensberger, Boyce, *et al.* "Media People on the New Science Boom." *SIPIscope*, September/October 1980, 2–9.

Sagan, Carl. *Cosmos*. New York: Random House, 1980.

_____. "Growing Up With Science Fiction." *New York Times Magazine*, 28 May 1978, 111–113.

_____. " 'There's No Hint of the Joys of Science.' " *TV Guide*, 4 February 1978, 6–8.

"Sagan's Metaphysical Parable." *Society*, July/August 1981, 91–95.

Slatzman, Joe. "MDs On TV: Are Their Video House Calls Bad Medicine?" *TV Guide*, 30 June 1979, 6–10.

Science Media Conference (special double issue). *The Exploratorium*, 5:2, 3 (1981).

"Science, Technology, and the Press: Must the 'Age of Innocence' End?" *Technology Review*, March/April 1980, 46–56.

Siegel, Mark. "Science-Fiction Characterization and TV's Battle for the Stars." *Science-Fiction Studies* 7 (1980): 270–277.

Solomon, Douglas S. "Health Campaigns on Television." *Television and Behavior: Ten Years of Scientific Progress and Implications for the Eighties, Vol. 2: Technical Reviews*, David Pearl, Lorraine Bouthilet, and Joyce Lazar, eds. Rockville, Md.: National Institute of Mental Health, 1982, 308–321.

Storm, Betsy. "Science Magazines: A Lively Reaction to Consumers' Thirst for Knowledge." *Madison Avenue*, July 1980, 27–36.

Sutherland, Zena. "For Young Readers—Science Books are Better Than Ever." *American Libraries*, October 1981, 535–539.

Television and Science (special issue). *CTW International Research Notes* 3 (Spring 1980).

Thomson, Peggy. "A TV Series Starring Science." *American Education*, March 1980, 7–13.

Tyrrell, W.B. "*Star Trek*'s Myth of Science." *Journal of American Culture* 2 (1979): 288–89.

Weiner, Jonathan. "Prime Time Science." *The Sciences* 20 (September 1980): 6–11.

WGBH-TV, Boston. *NOVA: Adventures in Science*. Reading, Mass.: Addison-Wesley, 1983.

Wilson, Robert R. "The New Literature of Science." *The Bulletin of the Atomic Scientists* 37 (April 1981): 1.

Wolff, Kathryn; Fritsche, Joellen; and Gross, Elina, comps. and eds. *The Best Science Books for Children*. Washington, D.C.: American Association for the Advancement of Science, 1983.

Wolff, Kathryn; Fritsche, Joellen M.; and Todd, Gary T., comps. and eds. *The Best Science Films, Filmstrips, and Videocassettes for Children*. Washington, D.C.: American Association for the Advancement of Science, 1983.

Zoglin, Richard. "Science on TV—How Sharp is the Focus?" *The New York Times*, 26 April 1981, D31.

PERIODICALS

This is a selected list of journals and magazines about science and technology, science teaching, and science for children.

American Scientist
bimonthly; $24
Scientific Research Society of North America
345 Whitney Ave.
New Haven, CT 06511

A general science journal with articles by prominent scientists and scholars.

Appraisal: Science Books for Young Children
3 issues a year; $12
Children's Science Book Review Committee
36 Cummington St.
Boston, MA 02215

Science books for children and adolescents reviewed by both librarians and science specialists.

Bulletin of the Atomic Scientists
monthly; $25
Educational Foundation for Nuclear Science
1020-24 E. 58th St.
Chicago, IL 60637

A science and public affairs magazine for general readers.

Discover: The Newsmagazine of Science
monthly; $22
Editorial:
Time Inc.
3435 Wilshire Blvd.
Los Angeles, CA 90010

Subscriptions:
Time-Life Building
541 North Fairbanks Court
Chicago, IL 60611

An illustrated popular science magazine for nonscientists.

Enter
10 issues a year; $12.95
Editorial:
Children's Television Workshop
One Lincoln Plaza
New York, NY 10023
Subscriptions:
P.O. Box 2932
Boulder, CO 80321

A newsmagazine for ten- to sixteen-year-olds about computers, video games, and new technology.

High Technology
monthly; $21
38 Commercial Wharf
Boston, MA 02110

An illustrated business magazine about new technology.

Journal of Research in Science Teaching
9 issues a year; $68
John Wiley and Sons
605 Third Ave.
New York, NY 10016

A scholarly journal for researchers and teachers, published by the National Association for Research in Science Teaching.

Microkids
bimonthly; $15
133 5th Ave.
New York, NY 10003

A magazine for adolescents about computers.

National Geographic
monthly $15
National Geographic Society
17th and M Sts., NW
Washington, DC 20036

An illustrated popular magazine about the natural and social sciences.

National Geographic World
monthly; $8.95
National Geographic Society
17th and M Sts., NW
Washington, DC 20036

An illustrated magazine about natural history for children ages eight to twelve.

Natural History
monthly; $15
American Museum of Natural History
Central Park West at 79th St.
New York, NY 10024

An illustrated magazine on ecology and the natural sciences for general readers.

Odyssey: The Young People's Magazine of Astronomy and Outer Space
monthly; $14.95
Astromedia Corp.
625 E. St. Paul Ave.
P.O. Box 92788
Milwaukee, WI 53202

An illustrated magazine about astronomy, space, and science for children of elementary and junior high school age.

Omni Magazine
monthly; $24
Editorial:
Omni Publications International Ltd.
1965 Broadway
New York, NY 10023
Subscriptions:
P.O. Box 5700
Bergenfield, NJ 07621

An illustrated science fact and science fiction magazine for general readers.

Popular Mechanics
monthly: $11.97
Editorial:
Hearst Magazines
224 W. 57th St.
New York, NY 10019
Subscriptions:
P.O. Box 10064
Des Moines, IA 50350

An illustrated popular magazine about new developments in science and technology.

Popular Science
monthly: $13.94
Editorial:
Times Mirror Magazines, Inc.
380 Madison Ave.
New York, NY 10017
Subscriptions:
Popular Science Subscription Dept.
Boulder, CO 80322

An illustrated popular magazine about new developments in science and technology.

Ranger Rick's Nature Magazine
monthly; $10.50
National Wildlife Federation
1412 16th St., NW
Washington, DC 20036

An illustrated ecology magazine for ages five to twelve. A teacher's guide is available.

School Science and Mathematics
8 issues a year; $18
School Science and Mathematics Association
Bowling Green State University
126 Life Science Building
Bowling Green, OH 43403
A journal for science and mathematics teachers.

School Science Review
quarterly; £18
Association for Science Education
College Lane
Hatfield, Herts AL10 9AA
England
A journal on the study and teaching of science.

Science
weekly; $53 for individuals, $90 for institutions
American Association for the Advancement of Science
1515 Massachusetts Ave., NW
Washington, DC 20005
A magazine offering essays and articles on developments in the sciences, science research, and science and public policy.

Science Activities
quarterly; $25
Heldref Publications
4000 Albemarle St., NW
Washington, DC 20016
A classroom aid for elementary, junior high, and high school teachers.

Science and Children
8 issues a year; $20 for individuals, $25 for institutions

National Science Teachers Association
1742 Connecticut Ave., NW
Washington, DC 20009
An illustrated magazine offering ideas for elementary and junior high school science teachers.

Science and Public Policy
bimonthly; $124.80
Editorial:
IPC Business Press Ltd. (Sales and Distribution)
Oakfield House
Perry Mount Rd.
Haywards Heath, Sussex RH16 3DH
England
Subscriptions:
Butterworth Scientific Ltd.
Journals Division
Box 63
Westbury House
Bury St.
Guildford, Surrey GU2 5BH
England
An international report on science and its relation to public affairs.

Science Books & Films
5 issues a year; $17.50
American Association for the Advancement of Science
1515 Massachusetts Ave., NW
Washington, DC 20005
Reviews science materials for various ages and audiences.

Science Digest
monthly; $13.97
Editorial:
888 Seventh Ave.
New York, NY 10106
Subscriptions:
P.O. Box 10076
Des Moines, IA 50350

A popular science magazine with brief articles on new developments in science and technology, intended for a general audience.

Science Education
5 issues a year; $40
John Wiley & Sons
605 Third Ave.
New York, NY 10016

A scholarly journal about research in science education at all levels.

Science 84
10 issues a year; $15
Editorial:
    1101 Vermont Ave., NW
    10th Floor
    Washington, DC 20005
Subscriptions:
    P.O. Box 10790
    Des Moines, IA 50340

An illustrated popular science magazine published by the American Association for the Advancement of Science "to bridge the distance between science and citizen." The title changes each year; i.e., *Science 83, Science 84*, etc.

Science News
weekly; $27.50
Editorial:
    Science Service, Inc.
    1719 N St., NW
    Washington, DC 20036
Subscriptions:
    231 West Center St.
    Marion, OH 43302

An illustrated summary of new developments in science and technology for general readers.

The Science Teacher
9 issues a year; $28

National Science Teachers Association
1742 Connecticut Ave., NW
Washington, DC 20009

A magazine for educators about the teaching of high school science.

Science, Technology, and Human Values
quarterly; $12 for individuals, $22 for institutions
MIT Press
28 Carleton St.
Cambridge, MA 02142

An academic journal about the relationship between science and society.

Science World
18 issues a year; $5
Scholastic Magazines, Inc.
50 W. 44th St.
New York, NY 10036

An illustrated magazine for science students in grades seven through ten. A teacher's guide is available.

Scientific American
monthly; $24
415 Madison Ave.
New York, NY 10017

An illustrated general science magazine for both scientists and nonscientists. The December issues contain an annual review of children's books on science.

Smithsonian Magazine
monthly; $17
Editorial:
    Smithsonian Associates
    900 Jefferson Dr., SW
    Washington, DC 20560
Subscriptions:
    Membership Data Center
    P.O. Box 2953
    Boulder, CO 80321

An illustrated popular magazine about science, technology, and ecology, among other subjects.

Technology Review
8 issues a year; $24
Massachusetts Institute of Technology
Room 10-140
Cambridge, MA 02139

An illustrated magazine for both scientists and nonscientists that explores new developments in science and technology.

3-2-1 Contact
10 issues a year; $10.95
Editorial:
  Children's Television Workshop
  One Lincoln Plaza
  New York, NY 10023
Subscriptions:
  P.O. Box 2933
  Boulder, CO 80321

A science magazine for ages eight to fourteen, related to the Children's Television Workshop TV series of the same name.

ORGANIZATIONS

This is a selected list of organizations concerned with science in general, science and the media, and science education. For information on organizations in specific fields of science, consult *Encyclopedia of Organizations* or contact the National Referral Center, Library of Congress, Washington, DC 20540, (202) 287-5670.

Academy of Applied Science (AAS)
Two White St.
Concord, NH 03301
(603) 225-2072

A scientific and educational group that works to encourage creativity in applied science.

American Association for the Advancement of Science (AAAS)
1515 Massachusetts Ave., NW
Washington, DC 20005
(202) 467-4400

A general science organization with committees on all branches of science.

American Council on Science and Health (ACSH)
1995 Broadway
New York, NY 10023
(212) 362-7044

An organization that works to influence public policies on health and the environment by encouraging more scientific input.

American Science Film Association (ASFA)
3624 Science Center
Philadelphia, PA 19104
(215) 387-2255

Scientists, educators, and film producers and distributors concerned with using film, television, and related media to communicate about science.

Association for the Education of Teachers in Science (AETS)
Department of Curriculum and Instruction
Old Dominion University
Norfolk, VA 23508
(804) 440-3283

An organization of supervisors of science teachers, from elementary school through college level.

Association for Women in Science (AWIS)
1346 Connecticut Ave., NW
Room 1122
Washington, DC 20036
(202) 833-1998

An organization of professional women and students in the sciences that works to promote equal opportunities for women in the sciences and to help women achieve their career goals.

Association of Science Museum Directors (ASMD)
Cleveland Museum of Natural History
University Circle
Cleveland, OH 44106
(216) 231-4600

An organization of chief administrative officers of science and social science museums.

Association of Science-Technology Centers (ASTC)
1016 16th St., NW
Washington, DC 20036
(202) 452-0655

An organization of science and technology museums that works to improve science and technology centers and to advance their role in society.

Center for Science in the Public Interest (CSPI)
1755 S St., NW
Washington, DC 20009
(202) 332-9110

A national nonprofit membership organization concerned with problems relating to nutrition and health.

Council for Elementary Science International (CESI)
c/o National Science Teachers
  Association
1742 Connecticut Ave., NW
Washington, DC 20009
(202) 328-5800

An organization that works to improve the teaching of science at all levels of elementary school.

Council for the Advancement of Science Writing (CASW)
618 N. Elmwood
Oak Park, IL 60302
(312) 383-0820

A private organization operated by a council of science writers, television executives, and scientists who work to promote science writing and a closer relationship between science and the press.

Essentia
Salina Star Route
Boulder, CO 80302
(303) 443-3484

An educational group that seeks to involve students in the study of the environment.

Federation for Unified Science Education (FUSE)
231 Battelle Hall of Science
Capital University
Columbus, OH 43209
(614) 236-6816

An organization of science teachers working to improve elementary and high school science education.

Federation of American Scientists (FAS)
307 Massachusetts Ave., NE
Washington, DC 20002
(202) 546-3300

An organization of scientists, engineers, and others concerned with problems of science and society.

Institute for Scientific Information (ISI)
3501 Market St.
University City Science Center
Philadelphia, PA 19104
(215) 386-0100

An information management company that collects and organizes scientific information.

International Council of Scientific Unions (ICSU)
51 Boulevard de Montmorency
F-75016 Paris, France

An organization of national research councils and scientific unions that coordinates scientific research done by national and international scientific unions.

National Academy of Sciences (NAS)
Office of Information
2101 Constitution Ave., NW
Washington, DC 20418
(202) 334-2000

A private organization of scientists and engineers working to promote science and its use for the general welfare.

National Association for Research in Science Teaching (NARST)
c/o Dr. William G. Holliday
NARST-EDCI
University of Calgary
Calgary, Alberta T2N 1N4
Canada
(403) 284-7485

An organization of science educators that promotes research in science education.

National Association of Academies of Science (NAAS)
Dept. of Physics
University of Mississippi
University, MS 38677
(601) 232-7046

An organization coordinating the activities of state and regional academies of science.

National Association of Science Writers (NASW)
P.O. Box 294
Greenlawn, NY 11740
(516) 757-5664

An organization of science writers and editors involved with communicating science news to the public.

National Institute of Science (NIS)
c/o Dr. L. Shelbert Smith
Dept. of Chemistry
Central State University
Wilberforce, OH 45384
(513) 376-6424

An organization of science teachers and college and university students.

National Network of Minority Women in Science (MWIS)
Office of Opportunities in Science
American Association for the Advancement of Science
1776 Massachusetts Ave., NW
Washington, DC 20036
(202) 467-5431

An organization that promotes the advancement of minority women in science fields.

National Research Council (NRC)
Office of Information
2101 Constitution Ave., NW
Washington, DC 20418
(202) 334-2000

An organization associated with the National Academy of Sciences, that researches scientific and technical data and administers funds for research projects and fellowships.

National Science for Youth Foundation (NSYF)
763 Silvermine Rd.
New Canaan, CT 06840
(203) 966-5643

An organization that sponsors natural science centers and nature museums.

National Science Foundation (NSF)
1800 G St., NW
Washington, DC 20550
(202) 357-7748

An independent agency of the federal government that funds research and education in the sciences.

National Science Supervisors Association (NSSA)
c/o Robert Fariel
113 Branch Ave.
Freeport, NY 11520
(516) 378-7686

An organization of supervisors of science teachers that works to improve science education.

National Science Teachers Association (NSTA)
1742 Connecticut Ave., NW
Washington, DC 20009
(202) 328-5800

An organization of teachers working to foster excellence in science education.

School Science and Mathematics Association (SSMA)
126 Life Science Building
Bowling Green State University
Bowling Green, OH 43403
(419) 372-0151

An organization of science and mathematics teachers of all levels that promotes science and mathematics education.

Science for the People (SFTP)
897 Main St.
Cambridge, MA 02139
(617) 547-0370

An organization of scientists, engineers, and others striving to make science responsive to human needs.

Science Talent Search (STS)
Science Service
1719 N St., NW
Washington, DC 20036
(202) 785-2255

A competition held by Science Service, a nonprofit group that encourages the public understanding of science, to discover and reward the scientific skills of high school seniors.

Scientists' Institute for Public Information (SIPI)
355 Lexington Ave.
New York, NY 10017
(212) 661-9110

A national nonprofit organization dedicated to increasing public awareness and understanding of issues involving science and public policy.

Union of Concerned Scientists (UCS)
1384 Massachusetts Ave.
Cambridge, MA 02138
(617) 547-5552

A nonprofit organization of scientists, engineers, and other professionals concerned about the impact of advanced technology on society.

INDEX